Baby Animals

Originally published as *Baby Animals*
© 2007 by L&P LLP

This 2009 edition published by Metro Books
by arrangement with L&P LLP

Jacket Design: Alex Ingr

Design Layout: Alastair Alexander

Project Editor: Ruth Urborn

Art Editor: David Fraser

Production and Editorial Manager: Karen Lomax

Author: Debbie Stowe

Metro Books
122 Fifth Avenue
New York, NY 10011

ISBN: 978-1-4351-1819-5

A catalog record for this title is available from the Library of Congress

Printed and bound in Malaysia

1 3 5 7 9 10 8 6 4 2

L&P LLP has made every effort to ensure that the content of this book is accurate at the time of production.
The publisher, authors and editors cannot be held liable for any errors or omissions in this publication or actions that
may be taken as a consequence of using it.

Baby Animals

DEBBIE STOWE

METRO BOOKS
NEW YORK

Contents

Introduction

The appeal of baby animals is not limited simply to children. Adults the world over have been charmed by the young versions of familiar creatures. Many traditional "fairy stories" have as their central characters young animals discovering the world around them. Whether this discovery is the three little pigs' attempts to build a home safe from the hungry wolf, or the drab duckling finding out that he is, in fact, a beautiful swan, baby animals serve as the players in many stories from history. Their role as explorers has not passed, however, as even in modern times the trend has carried on. *Piglet* has summoned up his courage to search for "heffalumps" with *Winnie-the-Pooh*, *Paddington Bear* has adventured with the Brown family to wherever he can carry his suitcase, and *Babe* has gone from snuffling in a pigsty to exploring the big city.

While the young of any animal can be appealing, they cannot survive on their looks alone. Many species face serious challenges to their existence from a wide range of threats, ranging from climate change taking away the habitat of polar bears, to genetic defects leaving cheetahs unlikely to survive into adulthood.

This book also details such information as the gestation time of the various animals—from the almost two year pregnancy of an elephant to the 60-day gestation period of a guinea pig—and the hazards presented to the parents of these babies—such as the challenges confronted by a mother dolphin or whale giving birth underwater. Even as it begins, the life of a young animal is far from easy.

Through the years, animals and their young have been the subject of poetry and prose, sculpture and painting, and every form of artistic expression known. Whether this has been the cartoon representations depicted in classic films, or poetic tributes from a Poet Laureate, you will find references to those tributes here. The charm and innocence of baby animals has a universal appeal and this book will go some way to explaining this, as well as providing information you may not have known before about these delightful and gentle creatures.

Read on, and enjoy discovering more about the start of life for so many beloved creatures.

Bears

Bears have succeeded in infiltrating the public consciousness like no other member of the animal kingdom. Their appearance, especially their young, can induce cries of affection from adults and children alike.

The impulse to care for one's young is a driving evolutionary force, the bedrock of survival. So strong is this urge that is transcends species: even the newborn of the most repulsive animal can evoke a protective flicker in a person, eliciting the "awww!" response. Weak, vulnerable, helpless—the baby tugs our emotions. And few babies are born more vulnerable than the bear cub. It may seem ironic that such a feeble offspring should come from the bear, the colossal mammal more usually linked with adjectives like grizzly and ferocious. But when it emerges, the size of a small rodent, the bear cub is toothless, blind (as it will remain for three weeks), almost bald, and entirely dependent on its mother.

Even to reach this state of utter helplessness is an achievement. Bears are born during the mother's hibernation. When she goes into her den, she will already be pregnant, sometimes with up to three or four cubs. Her weight is crucial to their survival: if she has not managed to eat enough to coat herself in sufficient fat,

A bear may grow up to be one of the most fearsome wild animals, but cubs are far less robust.

The odds of survival are still stacked against them. Around one half will die before they reach their first birthday.

they won't make it. The lucky ones are born after a couple of months, deep in the middle of winter.

But perhaps the maternal instinct of the female bear—renowned for her ferocity in seeing off any potential intruders when she feels her cubs are threatened—has not yet kicked in: despite her offspring's precarious, against-the-odds battle to be born, she will not even wake up for the birth itself. When it emerges into the world, the cub has to muster all its strength to wriggle into a nursing position, so it can start to feed on the nourishing elixir of its mother's milk. And it is very nourishing: the milk of the female brown bear is high in fat and calories—ten times as nutritional as cow's milk—and her young charges enjoy a growth spurt of such speed that by the time spring comes, they can walk out of their winter refuge and face the outside world.

The emergence of mother and child is in stark contrast. Feeding hungry mouths, especially if she has given birth to three or four cubs, takes its toll on the female's resources, as does the hibernation period, during which a bear's heart rate can drop from 40 beats per minute to a mere eight. During hibernation, the mother will most likely not have relieved herself for months; nor will she have had any exercise. Bears survive their fast thanks to the huge amount of food they take in before they bed down for winter. The bear could be described as the original binge eater, eating almost every waking hour. A brown bear can eat up to 90 pounds (40 kg) in a day in the fall, in preparation for the big sleep.

Around half of the baby bears born will not reach their first birthday, with starvation and disease the chief causes of mortality.

Quite understandably, after waking from such a period of dormancy, the mother is sluggish and lethargic. Her cubs, on the other hand, are infused with the excitement of discovery. For the first time, they are seeing things other than a dark den, their mother, and siblings. The trees, the land, the snow, the sky—everything is fresh and exhilarating. They delight in their newfound liberty of movement, fooling around with each other, jumping and climbing. The earth is their playground, as they fashion slides out of hills, gamboling and frolicking with joy.

Not that they are now on easy street. The odds of survival are still stacked against them. Around half will die before they reach their first birthday. Some are killed by lack of food; others will be struck down by disease. Mountain lions, wolves, coyotes, cougars—even other adult male bears are among the potential dangers, preying on young cubs who become separated from their mothers. Most horribly, a young cub can even be killed by its own father, who plays no part in rearing his young and can view them as rivals for his mate's attention. But their chances are boosted by their attentive mother, who devotes every physical resource and ounce of ferociousness to protecting her babies. Often she will have to take risks to ensure their survival. Because fellow bears are such a threat, the mother will lead her brood to an area where others are unlikely to be found.

That means heading for somewhere far away, where food is scarcer. While she protects her cubs from attack by one of their own, at the same time she exposes them to the perils of starvation. There is one other factor that can often ensure a relative absence of adult males: human beings.

Bears naturally shy away from people, which makes the borders of towns a tempting habitat. But by relocating to the vicinity of an urban area, where food is plentiful and rivals scarce, the mother puts her family in the path of one of its other predators: us. Raising young bears is a series of tough decisions, but the mother knows that the survival of her offspring depends upon making the right ones. And it's a high-stakes game: black bears usually reproduce every two years, brown bears every three or four. Her young are precious, and she is wholly committed to their endurance.

Bears are solitary creatures by nature. A *sleuth* of bears is their collective noun, but you will seldom see such a thing outside of a dictionary. This love of seclusion, however, is not evident at the beginning of a cub's life. Before the cub learns to forage, hunt, and fend for himself—and before the mother needs to switch her attention to the next litter—the baby will stick determinedly to his mother and she to him. For the first year of a cub's life, the mother will continue to feed him the wholesome milk that starts him on his journey from a blind, bald baby of around a

pound (0.45 kg), in the case of brown bears, to a fully grown adult weighing over a thousand times as much. In the early days, the new family will cling to the den and the security it affords, sometimes even sleeping in it. Even when the time is right to move on from their birthplace, the cubs will rarely venture more than a couple of hundred yards from the protective matriarch. They stay within the reassuring cocoon of their single-parent family for anything from 18 months to four-and-a-half years. At the age of around three to four, the black female reaches sexual maturity, her brown counterpart three years later, and the cycle is ready to begin all over again.

Humankind's relationship with the bear has

The president took pity on his helpless captive and released the bear, from a sense of fair play.

long been close but ambivalent: we have both embraced the creature and imbued it with negative stereotypes. In financial trading jargon, a bear market means that prices are falling, and a negative economic outlook is described as "bearish," said to be owing to the bear's tendency to look downwards. The term *bearish* also means grumpy, with bad-tempered people often compared with the proverbial "bear with a sore head." But while adult bears are considered grouchy and fierce, the babies of the species have entered our cultural consciousness in a far more benign way. How much more loved, accepted, and trusted can an animal become than the first toy of children all over the world?

The origins of the humble teddy bear—a symbol of simplicity and innocence in today's age of high-tech toys—are no less than presidential. Now part of American myth, there are various versions of the tale. One has it that Theodore Roosevelt was big-game hunting in Colorado. He failed to make a kill, and as a consolation, the maids of the Hotel Colorado in Glenwood Springs gave him a makeshift bear, which they had put together from odd pieces of material. His daughter later named the bear Teddy. But the more popular version—perhaps because it communicates the President's compassion, rather than his lack of luck as a hunter—comes from Sharkey County, Mississippi. This legend has it that Holt Collier, the famed African-American hunter, had caught and bound a bear for Roosevelt to shoot. The President took pity on his helpless captive and released the bear, out of a sense of fair play.

While a mother bear emerges sluggish from hibernation, her newborn exhibits an awed curiosity and delight in its new surroundings, such as this black bear (Ursus americanus), intrigued by a striped skunk.

The episode was immediately seized upon by the press, but with the newspaper cartoonists turning the animal from a wretched old bear into a young cub, to ratchet up the drama.

The incident happened in 1902. Over a hundred years later, teddy bears are found in homes all over the world. And they have earned the love of the public perhaps more than any other toy, with young and old alike both smitten. While children's bears are used in rough-and-tumble games (a bear is much more durable than a Playstation) for dressing up and for cuddles when required, other bears have become artistic or antique collector items and the owning adult is unlikely to let a child get its hands on that precious bear. Globally, devotees celebrate the teddy: teddy bear museums can be found in Korea, Japan and Hong Kong, the United States, and over much of Europe. The United States and United Kingdom seem to be particularly fond of the toy.

Perhaps because of the animal's human-like characteristics, such as its propensity to stand on two legs, which is relatively rare among mammals, bears have appeared frequently in literature, with young ones proving particularly inspiring to writers and enduring among readers. *Paddington Bear*, created by British author Michael Bond over 50 years ago, was born when Bond spotted a forlorn looking teddy on a shelf in a London shop on Christmas Eve and brought it home for his wife. Unlike his real life counterparts, who are omnivores, feeding themselves with whatever grasses, fungi, nuts, sprouts, berries and roots they can find, occasionally supplemented by fish, insects and small mammals, fussy *Paddington* was partial to marmalade sandwiches.

Rupert the Bear is another UK creation, and started life in a newspaper comic strip in 1920. He was followed later that decade by *Winnie-the-Pooh*, who was to become one of Walt

Smokey was so popular he was even awarded his own zip code for all the fan mail he was getting.

Bears have only one natural enemy: Humankind. In North America, the arrival of European settlers heralded the bear's demise. Human expansion has cut into the animal's habitat and food sources, pushing it closer to the danger of urban areas.

Disney's most successful characters. The character was created by British writer A.A. Milne, who wrote stories about his son, Christopher Robin, and a teddy he owned. The toy was named after a female black bear cub that the Milnes often saw on their visits to London Zoo, called Winnipeg. Her story merited attention in its own right, and eventually got it with the 2004 movie *A Bear Named Winnie*. Winnipeg was purchased for $20 by Lieutenant Harry Colebourn, who was serving as the veterinarian for the Fort Garry Horse Canadian regiment of cavalry, on their way to fight in France during World War I. Charmed by the bear, the regiment snuck her into the United Kingdom as their mascot. Colebourn deposited her safely at London Zoo before the soldiers headed across the English channel for the French battlefields. Playful and gentle, Winnipeg never attacked anyone, and

it was these qualities that enchanted the author and his son. A statue of the cub with Lieutenant Colebourn now stands in Assiniboine Park in the Canadian city whose name she shares.

As well as entertaining generations of children, baby bears have been adopted into the educational process. The United States Forest Service has used Smokey Bear as its mascot for decades. He has a real-life counterpart: a black bear cub who escaped the 1950 Capitan Gap fire in New Mexico by hanging onto a tree. After being rescued with only burnt paws, the bear was taken home by a local rancher who had been assisting the firefighters, and later found a home in the National Zoo, Washington DC, where he lived for over a quarter of a century. Smokey was so popular he was even awarded his own zip code for all the fan mail he was getting. The royalties his image earned were plowed back into forest fire prevention education, in what is the longest-running public-service campaign in American history. He is buried in the New Mexico historical park that was set up to commemorate him and named after him. Another famous bear cub mascot was Misha, the symbol of the 1980 Olympic Games in Moscow, and the first such character to play an extensive role in promoting the Games.

But while we have embraced the bear in our literature and culture, humankind's increasing use of the planet's resources is threatening it. Bears have only one natural enemy: us. In North America, their decline began almost as soon as the first European settlers arrived. Within a century, the population

of brown bears had fallen to a tenth of where it started. As we have built roads, chopped down trees, and expanded our towns and cities, we have continued to shrink the bear's habitat and reduce its sources of food, forcing the creatures into urban areas to forage. With this, they have become increasingly used to humans, resulting in the face-to-face confrontations that harm both human and animal. Collisions with vehicles have also become common. In some parts of the Middle East, the brown bear is regionally extinct. Some black bears also have endangered status.

In China, Korea and Vietnam, where pressing human concerns allow little room for animal rights to take root, bears are farmed. Their bile is used in Chinese medicine and now in some shampoos. Bear gall bladders are also illegally traded, and sellers can charge up to 18 times their weight in gold, according to Harvard's Center for Health and the Global Environment. In many countries hunting bears is legal—which is not to say that it does not go on in other countries too. The bear's remote habitat makes policing their hunting almost impossible.

Thanks to the efforts of environmentalists, the numbers of bears are rising again in certain areas, and in some cases they are being removed from the endangered list. It is typical of our love-hate relationship with the creatures that while some of us fight for the bear's survival, others kill it for sport or for money. The child who goes to sleep with his teddy bear tucked under his arm may one day become the man who stalks the bear with his gun.

Cats

Cats have lived alongside mankind for thousands of years, and have become part of our lives and culture.

Born almost helpless, kittens mature within weeks into playful explorers of their surroundings.

Few baby animals convey vulnerability as effortlessly as the kitten. Born deaf, blind, and helpless, unable to relieve itself without stimulation, and incapable of regulating its own body temperature, a newborn kitten is wholly dependent on its mother for survival. And a conscientious mother is essential, particularly in cold climates: If the temperature goes below 80°F (27°C), an unprotected kitten can die from exposure. Its skin is loose, allowing the mother to carry her brood using her teeth. For a week, maybe a week and a half, their eyes remain closed. When they first open them, all cats' eyes are blue, and they slowly change color over the coming months. The cat's introduction to the world of sight is a gradual one: At first its retina is largely ineffective, and it takes around three months until it can see as well as an adult. About the same time as a kitten's eyes open, its closed ear canals also begin to unlock. Soon, it can relieve itself independently and regulate its temperature, too.

But it is those first few weeks of helplessness that are impinged on the public consciousness. The kitten is just five inches (12 cm) long at birth and weighs between two and four ounces (55–110 g). Its tininess and vulnerability so touch human hearts, that in children's literature, a stock villainous act is to cast a bag of squirming kittens into the water to drown them. Bumbling British butler Edgar, from the Disney film *The Aristocats*, is thwarted in his attempts to commit this heinous act.

On top of their fragility, we also love kittens for their irresistible cuteness, a cuteness that has informed popular culture and even infiltrated the vernacular. In the fashion world, the term "kitten heel" describes a woman's shoe with a short and slender heel, typically between 1.5 and 2 inches (3–5 cm) high. Apparently so-called because the curve of the heel resembles a kitten's claw, the style was pioneered by Audrey Hepburn in the 1950s. The previous decade gave birth to the phrase "sex kitten," applied to women who

We love kittens for their irresistible cuteness, a cuteness that has informed popular culture and even infiltrated the vernacular.

appeared to have both a kitten's cuteness and its sprightly energy.

Kittens are poster favorites—peeking out of a shoe, draped over the head or under the ear of a big dog, or wearing a pair of shades—and frequently feature in home videos, jumping up to reach a door handle or engaged in some other domestic mischief. Their curiosity makes them perfect entertainment. French author Jules Champfleury sums it up: "There is no more an intrepid explorer than a kitten." William

Wordsworth, the English Romantic poet, was so charmed by kittens' antics, that he wrote several poems about the creatures. In *The Kitten and the Falling Leaves*, he observes:

But the Kitten, how she starts,
Crouches, stretches, paws, and darts!
First at one, and then its fellow
Just as light and just as yellow;

His contemporary, the Irish novelist Lady Sydney Morgan, often found them superior to human company, commenting: "The playful kitten, with its pretty little tigerish gambols, is infinitely more amusing than half the people one is obliged to live with in the world."

But while their inquisitiveness and energy have captivated the imagination of writers, these delightful qualities can also get them into trouble: kittens love hiding in small dark places and can easily get stuck. From helpless babies, within two weeks they reach the feline equivalent of the terrible twos, play-fighting, pouncing, and clawing, learning the basics survival skills from their mother. Their cuteness is juxtaposed with a ruthless hunter's mind: even the domestic kitty shares the predatory traits of its relatives in the jungle. Kittens complement

their agility with a keen sense of hearing, sight, and smell, and practice pouncing and clawing—to the detriment of many a piece of furniture. A growing cat will often be eager to show off its nascent hunting skills, proudly dragging a dead mouse into the house to present triumphantly to its owner. This is another replica of the jungle behavior of big cats, who present their prey to their peers in the den in a feline social gesture. But cats can be prey as well as predator. The kitten's wits are also put to use protecting itself from the occasional vicious dog or fox, and the loose skin that enables it to be carried around by its mother is also a useful escape mechanism: In the event it is seized by a predator, the cat can often wriggle free, suffering only a slight loss of fur.

Kittens complement their agility with a keen sense of hearing, sight, and smell, and practice pouncing and clawing—to the detriment of many a piece of furniture.

"Kittens are born with their eyes shut. They open them in about six days, take a look around, then close them again for the better part of their lives," declared cat expert and writer Stephen Baker

The kitten's cuteness has made it a favorite on art prints and greeting cards. Siamese kittens (left), with their dark paws, face, and tail, are one of the most distinctive breeds.

Of course, all this hunting and frolicking takes energy, and kittens are also well known for another pastime—sleeping. As writer and cat expert Stephen Baker puts it: "Kittens are born with their eyes shut. They open them in about six days, take a look around, then close them again for the better part of their lives." Sleeping kittens are one of the most popular and endearing animal images—particularly when they clump. The clump is an efficient sleeping method where kittens pile on top of each other, both to keep warm through the conservation of body heat and for safety in numbers. When the kitten at the top of the pile starts to feel the chill, it will slide down and delve to the bottom, thus promoting its sibling to the top—and the cycle begins again. In the early days and cold climates, this warmth conservation is an essential tool against the elements.

So enticing is the image of the napping kitty that it became one of America's most successful corporate symbols. Chessie started life as an etching in a 1933 newspaper, a dozing kitten languidly extending a paw from under a blanket.

L.C. Probert, who worked in PR and advertising for the Chesapeake & Ohio Railway, was at the time working on a campaign to advertise his company's new air-conditioned sleeper service, and deemed the contented kitten just the image to help him. With the slogan "Sleep Like a Kitten and Wake Up Fresh as a Daisy in Air-Conditioned Comfort," the ad made its first appearance in *Fortune* magazine in September 1933. Chessie, who at that point was still nameless, was not

an American feline: the artist responsible for the original etching hailed from Vienna, Austria. Guido Gruenwald, who specialized in cats as well as other animals, was paid $5 for the rights to use his creation. Chessie (an abbreviation of Chesapeake) was a big hit, starring in her own catalogue in 1934 which had an impressive print run of 40,000 copies. "America's Sleepheart," as she became known, soon got a couple of doubles and a mate called Peake. Not only did she make the advertising campaign a huge success, she also boosted public morale in Depression-era America, and was subsequently used during World War II, when she altruistically gave up her berth to traveling soldiers. Her longevity is comparable to that other American advertising icon, the Marlborough Man: Chessie was still hard at work promoting the railway after the

Amtrak takeover in the 1970s. Today, though no longer in active service, the perennial kitten has retained her place in the nation's affections, and her memorabilia is a popular collector's item.

Ironically, given the success of the slumberous Chessie and stereotype of napping cats, kittens are not prone to long periods of deep sleep. Nighttime is when a cat has the best chance of catching rodents, so this is when it is most active. And with their own predators to worry about—as a biological impulse, if not a reality in a closeted suburban home—they cannot risk making themselves vulnerable by

indulging in too deep a sleep. Kittens' reluctance to head for bed is described in Beatrix Potter's century-old *The Tale of Tom Kitten*, where Tom and his siblings are sent to their rooms by their mother as punishment for losing their best clothes: "She sent them upstairs; and I am sorry to say she told her friends that they were in bed with the measles—which was not true. Quite the contrary; they were not in bed: Not in the least. Somehow there were very extraordinary noises overhead, which disturbed the dignity and repose of the tea party."

Tom's mother Tabitha Twitchit had only three

troublesome kittens to deal with. Her real life counterpart is likely to give birth to many more over the course of her lifetime. The average cat litter is between two and seven kittens—but the record is 19. Gestation lasts between 60 and 70 days. Unchecked, a cat can produce a new litter every four months. Factoring in a female cat's fertile years, this adds up to quite a numerous brood: Over seven years, a single feline couple could theoretically generate 420,000 descendants. Dusty, a tabby cat, is believed to be the super-mom of the cat world, having produced an

While kittens' behavior is often endearing, they share many of the instincts of their wild cousins. Many an item of furniture falls victim to small claws, and few felines can understand their owners' lack of enthusiasm at the delivery of a dead mouse.

impressive 420 kittens. And taking the prize for longevity is Kitty, whose two kittens, born when their mother was 30, completed a documented tally of 218. Fortunately, the maternal duties are not necessarily protracted: Some kittens will be sent off to fend for themselves at the age of just three months. To prevent a feline invasion, owners commonly spay and neuter their pets. Even so, an estimated 35,000 kittens are born every day in the United States. In one quirk of cat conception, the litter may be half-siblings, rather than full. Female cats are what is known as "super fecund," meaning that the kittens born in one litter can have different fathers.

But while cats may be abundant, and lack the scarcity factor of other favorites, such as the panda, kittens have still collected some famous fans. British wartime Prime Minister Sir Winston Churchill's kitten was privileged enough to have a special chair, on which he sat while the statesman dined. His presence was a prerequisite, and servants were often dispatched to find the feline before dinner could begin. Jock was a ginger kitten, given to Churchill by his private secretary, Jock Colville, for whom he was named. The prized cat was on his master's deathbed in 1965. The Prime Minister stipulated the continued presence of a marmalade cat at his residence, Chartwell,

in his will, which saw Jock II and Jock III follow the original.

Like Wordsworth, who wrote several cat poems, English author Charles Dickens also developed an affection for a deaf kitten, known only as the "Master's Cat"—despite the cat's habit of extinguishing Dickens's candle to get the writer's attention, and thereby slowing progress on some of the most important novels in English literature. Eleanor Poe Barlow wrote a biography of Dickens from the viewpoint of the kitten: *The Master's Cat: The Story Of Charles Dickens As Told By His Cat.* Artists too have been inspired by kittens.

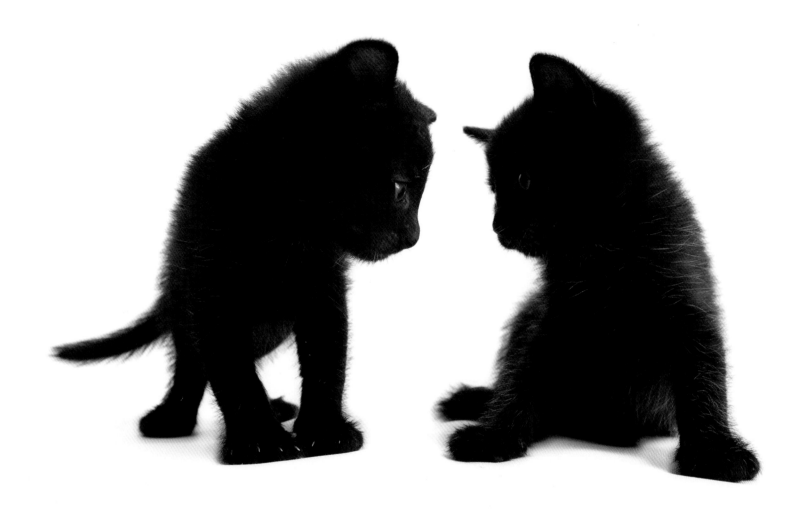

Leonardo da Vinci remarked: "The smallest feline is a masterpiece." Kittens even have their devotees in the animal kingdom. Koko, the Californian gorilla whom scientists from Stanford University have been teaching to communicate, has looked after several cats, and her loving relationship with kitten All Ball was written about in the 1987 book *Koko's Kitten*.

Of course, there are other figures who have not been so keen. When Napoleon Bonaparte was found on one occasion brandishing his sword vigorously and sweating with fear, the provocation was a kitten. Other famous ailurophobics—people with a fear of cats—are said to include fellow Frenchmen King Henry III and Louis XIV, Adolf Hitler, Mussolini, and Julius Ceasar.

But while cats have both their devotees and detractors, there are few hearts that do not melt at the sight of a kitten. Perhaps the humorous poet Ogden Nash sums it up best: "The trouble with a kitten is that when it grows up, it's always a cat."

Lucky or unlucky? Black cats are considered to herald either good or bad fortune depending on criteria as diverse as which way they are walking, who owns the cat, and which country you're in.

While the enmity between cats and dogs is legendary, they can in fact develop harmonious relations if they are introduced at a young age, which makes for some of the most endearing animal photographs.

Cheetahs

Cheetahs are the respected high speed hunters of the African plains. Uniquely camouflaged and highly agile these perfect hunters must pass on their abilities to their young to ensure their survival.

When the baby cheetah tumbles, blind, into the world, it faces depressing odds. Genetic similarity within the species, poachers, predators, and human encroachment on its habitat have conspired to reduce the cheetah cub's chance of survival to one in ten. Hence the irony that while the cheetah is the most reproductive cat, it now faces an uncertain future, with some experts doubting whether the species, the world's fastest land animal, is still viable.

The mother can give birth to up to eight cubs, but a typical litter is two to five. There is little sign of the animal's distinctive spots in newborns, as they are practically blended together. Nor has it yet taken on the normal sandy color: cheetah cubs have long dark fur. This is believed to be a disguise bestowed upon the vulnerable babies by evolution: Their coat gives them the aspect of the ratel, or honey badger, a fierce hunting animal that most predators wisely choose to leave to its own devices. It also offers the protection of camouflage, resembling the scorched grass typical of the cheetah's habitat, and protects the cub from wet and hot weather. But the defense is not an enduring one: from about three months old, the cub starts to lose this camouflage and must find other ways to defend itself in a hostile world.

Like other cats, cheetahs are born blind, toothless, and utterly dependent. Even before the birth, the mother must act against the many dangers facing her brood. She will give birth in

One of the lucky ones: A lack of genetic diversity, poachers, predators, and human encroachment have combined to reduce a newborn cheetah's survival odds to a depressing one in ten.

Like other cats, cheetahs are born blind, toothless, and utterly dependent. Their mother must ensure her family stay one step ahead of potential predators.

A cheetah mother must hunt for food for her young. As they accompany her, their inexperience can often alert potential prey.

a secluded place, then move the family from one new home to another, always ensuring they stay one step ahead of potential predators. In doing this she has no help. Male cheetahs play no part in rearing their offspring, and are long gone by this time. As a result, for the first six weeks the newborn cubs are left alone for long periods of time while their mother goes hunting. It is a perilous time in a cub's life, and, in the wild, around 90 percent will not make it.

For those that do, it will soon be time to go to school. From about two months old, the cubs accompany their mother on the hunt. However, they are by no means natural hunters and frequently thwart mom's efforts to snag that

day's meal. Many a gazelle is thrown a lifeline by a bored cub wandering ahead or playing with its siblings, alerting it to the impending attack of a determined matriarch. Back in the "classroom," the mother will attempt to inculcate a hunter's mentality in her young by bringing back injured prey for them to finish off. This training in the art of the kill is certainly a challenge—although it cannot be said that the small apprentices lack optimism. Young cheetahs will attempt to pursue "prey" that even an adult would have no hope of catching, like giraffes, far too big for any cheetah to claim, and birds, which simply avoid capture by flying away. They also learn through play, practicing their hunting moves on each other.

Some observers have noticed a gender divide: while female cubs go about their mission with effort, male ones can be lazy, waiting for mom and the sisters to feed them.

Hunting is just one set of essential life skills for the cheetah. The other is self-defense. They are prey as well as predator, and as the physically weakest of the big cat family, there is no shortage of creatures keen to snack on a cheetah cub. Other cats, such as lions and leopards, baboons, hyenas, jackals, even larger snakes and birds represent threats. The cheetah cannot match force with force. Its great asset is speed—a

cheetah can reach 70 miles (112 km) an hour. But this is also its vulnerability, as the small head, weak jaw, and small teeth that allow the animal to move so quickly are little help when self-defense is required. The so-called "greyhound of the cats," its best defense is always to run. It cannot risk injury, as any reduction in hunting prowess is likely to lead to starvation. Cubs can expect little protection from their mother. Much of the time she is away from the den, hunting, and even if she is nearby, she is powerless to fend off a large attacker such as a lion or a hyena. Some mothers even abandon their weaker cubs, finding that their

As the physically weakest of the cat family, there is no shortage of creatures ready to snack on a cheetah cub.

As both predator and prey, young cheetahs must take sleep when they can.

energy or the food is too stretched to nourish the whole brood—although a motherless cub will sometimes be taken in by another family.

Fellow animals are just one of the threats to the cheetah. A lack of genetic diversity—attributed to a fall in the population around 10,000 years ago—means that closely related animals have been breeding, leaving many cheetahs with weak immune systems rendering them prone to disease. Even in captivity, protected from would-be predators, 30 percent of cubs die within a month of being born. Some biologists now believe that the inbreeding is too extensive for the species to flourish.

The greatest danger, however, is humankind. The spread of farming and development have cut into the cheetah's natural habitat and reduced its potential food. This has driven the animal to seek alternative resources and feed on livestock, which has resulted in more confrontations with humans, from which the animal usually comes off worse. Poachers and hunters have also made inroads into the cheetah population, even though the animal is listed as an endangered species by the US Fish and Wildlife Service and protected by the Convention on International Trade of Endangered Species Treaty, and hunting it is illegal in many countries.

As a result, the cheetah population has been shrinking drastically, from 100,000 at the start of the 20th century to 25,000 in 1980 and today somewhere around half that number. Biologists believe that if its decline continues unchecked, the species could be extinct within a decade, a sad end for an animal that has been in existence for several million years. Many people are doing their best to prevent this. In the United States, cubs have been produced through artificial insemination, using reproductive materials from Namibian cheetahs, the most numerous and therefore offering the best genetic prospect of success.

Though often still inept hunters, cubs are abandoned by their mother when they reach 18 months, as she must start the cycle again with a new litter. If they are also abandoned by humans—left to hunters, poachers, animal predators, and their bleak genetic destiny—cheetah cubs may no longer be in nature guides, but in history books.

Although a cheetah will grow up to become the fastest land mammal, it is the weakest of the big cats. Cubs can also be inept hunters, often letting prey escape.

Chicks

Tiny and fluffy, baby chicks emerge from their eggs in a process that has come to represent creation itself. Their hatching has been adopted by both pagans and Christians as a symbol of new life and new hope, and is even the stuff of philosophical contemplation, through the classic causality question: Which came first, the chicken or the egg?

Given the symbolic importance of the chick-hen relationship, it is an irony that chicks do not need the devotion of their mother to survive and flourish. Though they may do slightly better with her attention, motherless chicks can manage quite well, and do not face the bleak future that many baby animals do when bereft of mom. Unlike other babies, they do not immediately demand food, and can live happily for a day, sometimes even two, without receiving any food. This is thanks to the wonderful nourishment provided by the yolk, which sustains the chick through its development, birth, and thereafter. In the egg, the cell is attached to the side of the

Most commonly associated with the Christian holiday of Easter, chicks are the perfect symbol of birth and renewal. These tiny, yellow downed young herald the arrival of spring, and are a favorite of children across the world.

The record number of yolks found in a hens egg is nine—which could have led, presumably, to a very well-fed and portly chick.

yolk, and feeds on it through a series of blood vessels. In the time leading up to the moment of hatching, the chick draws the rest of the yolk into its abdomen, via its umbilical cord, to ensure it will not go hungry when it reaches the outside world. Cooks are often pleased to crack open an egg and find two yolks inside it. In fact, the record number is nine—which could have led, presumably, to a very well-fed and portly chick.

Given the adorability of chicks, many people feel guilty eating eggs. But not all eggs could produce baby chicks—the eggs must first be fertilized by a rooster. Hens will continue to lay eggs regardless of whether this is the case or not. The gestation period is around three weeks. Individual eggs hatch separately, as the hen normally cannot lay more than one per day, although the record stands at an impressive

If a nesting hen senses any threat she will respond viciously, clucking and pecking—even black bears are said to turn and run when a protective mother hen is on the attack.

seven. The hen will sometimes take a break from laying eggs to concentrate on their incubation. During this period, she gives up almost all outside activities, including eating and drinking, to sit on her nest, guarding her brood. If she senses any threat she will respond viciously, clucking and pecking—giving the lie to the associations of chickens with cowardice. Even black bears are said to turn and run when a protective mother hen is on the attack. Some mothers, though, are better than others: the Cochin, Cornish, and Silkie breeds are particularly maternal. Not only is the mother required to maintain a constant temperature of over 100°F (38°C), she must also turn the eggs by at least 90 degrees, between three and five times a day. Without this rotation, the embryo could get stuck to the shell, which can result in birth defects. The embryonic chick is also protected by the egg white, which cradles it, softening the effect of any sudden movements or knocks.

Inside a hot and humid egg, it seems surprising that the chick has enough air to survive. But while the shell has the appearance of being solid, an egg that can be held comfortably in the human hand has a remarkable 8,000 pores that allow the chick to breathe. It was the Scottish doctor

The simplicity with which they represent the miracle of life and their associations with springtime have led chicks to symbolize rebirth, and the baby birds are commonly given as gifts at Easter time.

While chickens are not known for their airborne prowess, at two weeks old most baby chicks can manage to fly just over a foot.

Chicks hatch wet and barely able to move, but rapidly become mobile.

and amateur chemist John Davy who discovered this in 1863, when he pumped pressurized air into an egg that he had put underwater, to see a multitude of small bubbles rise to the surface. Three days before it is ready for its exit, the chick uses a small horn-shaped point on its beak to puncture the air cell at the bottom of the egg and breathe its first air direct from outside. This breath is the stimulus it needs to start peeping, or making a series of short, soft, high-pitched noises, to alert its mother to its impending arrival. When the mother hen senses the chick peeping in the egg, she will start clucking gently, encouraging her baby to break out of its shell and into the outside world. When they do emerge from the protective environs of the shell, the first thing that chicks need is neither food nor maternal attention—it is solitude. Wet and bedraggled, they are suffering

from the effects of 21 days cocooned in a small space, and for the first few hours they can barely move. But their mobility level soon develops. While chickens are not known for their airborne prowess, at two weeks old most baby chicks can manage to fly just over 12 inches (30 cm).

Perhaps because the baby chick will never reach the grace and proficiency of flight of many of its fellow birds, it has come to be associated with a certain endearing haplessness. In the modern version of an old fable thought to have originated in Indian folklore, Chicken Little is walking through the woods when an acorn falls on her head. She interprets this as proof that the sky is falling in, and spreads her message of panic through the village, causing chaos. The story is used to impart the moral that one should not believe everything one is told, and also to warn

As far back as pagan times, people believed that eggs were imbued with special powers. They buried them under buildings in the hope of keeping the occupants safe from harm.

against cowardice, which is so closely linked with the bird that calling someone a chicken is to call them a coward. The tale has inspired many retellings, including a 2005 Disney movie, in which *Chicken Little* is called upon to save the world.

But the most important symbolism connected to the chick is to do with rebirth. The simplicity and visibility of soft, warm life emerging from a hard egg has captured human imagination over the generations. As far back as pagan times, people believed that eggs were imbued with special powers. They buried them under buildings in the hope of keeping the occupants safe from harm. It was considered lucky for brides

to step on an egg before crossing the threshold and entering their new home. Eggs were given as gifts, lucky charms that would increase the recipient's fertility and family. They formed an important part of pagan fertility rituals, and as a result both eggs and chicks were associated with new life. Pagans derived their spirituality from the natural world, and involved chicks and eggs with the celebration of spring. Historians believe that as Christianity spread across Central Europe, these pagan spring rites fused with the Easter celebrations taking place around the same time, and early Christians adopted the egg and the chick as part of Easter celebrations.

Pagans derived their spirituality from the natural world, and involved chicks and eggs with the celebration of spring. Early Christians adopted the egg and the chick as part of Easter celebrations.

The very word *Easter* is descended from the Scandinavian word "Ostra" and Germanic word "Eastre," both of which were goddesses of spring and fertility. There was perfect synchrony with the Resurrection: just as Christ emerged alive from the tomb, so chicks emerge from the egg. Egg-rolling, symbolic of the rolling back of the boulder of Jesus's tomb, is still popular around Europe, and the Easter Egg Roll on the White House lawn has a history dating back over 135 years.

Chicks themselves are also an important part of Easter celebrations, and are commonly given as gifts and put on display. Some farms give a novel twist to the trend by injecting their eggs with a temporary nontoxic dye, which means that when the chicks hatch, they do so in a vivid rainbow of colors. Within a few weeks, as the chicks grow new feathers, they return to their natural hue, but in the meantime the multicolored results of the newborns delight the visiting children.

Because of their abundance—there are more chickens in the world than people—children come into frequent contact with baby chicks. They may not be the obvious choice for a pet, but chicks can be trained and tamed. They will eat out of your hand, may allow themselves to be stroked, and some even develop enough loyalty to follow their owner around. Their relative domesticity makes them ideal for human interaction, and hatching programs are on the curriculum in numerous schools as a means of teaching children about the miracle of life—although some groups condemn the practice as cruel, it is important that the developing eggs are properly tended and kept in the right conditions.

The simplicity with which they represent the miracle of life and their associations with springtime have led chicks to symbolize rebirth, and the baby birds are commonly given as gifts at Easter time.

Cows

Long revered as a sacred animal by some cultures, the cow has always had close associations with mankind. Their young calves have very strong connections with their mothers, in one of the strongest bonds found in nature.

A baby calf frolicking through a grassy field heralds the arrival of spring: sunny days, nature, youth, and optimism. But our relationship with the calf has been ambivalent, featuring both devotion and mistreatment since humans first began farming cattle several millennia ago. While past peoples have revered and worshipped the calf, throughout Biblical times it was commonly sacrificed to appease God for human sins. While that kind of practice is now largely in the past, the modern-day equivalent sees calves being

sacrificed instead on the altar of consumerism and decadence, to give us luxury garments and delicacies. And our reliance on the milk that cows produce for their offspring to nurture and nourish our own young complicates this dependent relationship even further.

Most calves are born in springtime, which is perhaps why their frolicking has come to be associated with that season in much the same way as the lamb. They are also associated with youth, sometimes in the form of the cherub,

creation, and generation. Like us, cows have a gestation period of nine months. But whereas a human baby emerges helpless and almost immobile, a calf comes into the world ready for action. A precocious species, the young can move around and recognize their mother almost immediately. Within a day a newborn calf can identify its mother's call. Nor is the newborn tiny—it weighs around 80 to 100 pounds (36 to 45 kg), and one poor British Friesian cow had to go through the ordeal of giving birth to a 225-

A newborn calf weighs around 80 to 100 pounds (36 to 45 kg), and one poor British Friesian cow had to go through the ordeal of giving birth to a 225-pound (102 kg) calf in 1961.

pound (102 kg) calf in 1961. The baby will almost immediately begin to feed from its mother's udder. Its first priority—and the priority of the female—is to make sure it gets enough of the immunity-boosting liquid called colostrum secreted by the mother—at least two liters within its first six hours and eight liters throughout the course of its first day. Without the energy, protein, and immunoglobulins in its mother's milk, its long-term health will be threatened, and it will not delight in playing and mixing with other calves, as is natural for the robust young of the species. Cows can continue to be suckled for several months. From the age of two or three, when a female cow reaches breeding age, she can typically have one baby a year. Twins are rare. The natural bovine lifespan is 20 years, and the cow that holds the record for longevity, a Dremon called Big Bertha, who passed away at 38 in 1993, is also listed as the most prolific mother, having given birth to 39 calves.

Big Bertha was apparently something of a special case. But earlier civilizations found much to respect in cows. The Hebrews, like other Jewish farming societies, were calf-worshippers, although the use of the term has economic rather than literal origins. It was not, in fact, young cows that they particularly held up as sacred, but that the representations they fashioned had to be small due to the unaffordability of metal; therefore the images came to be known as calves. As early as 1000 BC, the Egyptians also worshipped calves, although their devotions were to the live animal itself, rather than a manufactured representation, leading some historians to conclude that the two traditions were not connected. Even today, Hindus believe the cow is sacred and ancient Indian texts compare the gods' devotion to their followers to a cow's dedication to her calves. The Sikh holy book, the Guru Granth Sahib, also makes reference to the love between a cow and her young.

The calf also features frequently in the Bible, although generally in less pleasant circumstances. Because calves had been worshipped by non-Christians, they exerted a strong hold over some societies, and frequently tempted them away from Christian teachings and practice. In the Book of Kings, the King of Israel has two idol calves built, in order to keep the ten tribes from going to Jerusalem to worship. And in Exodus, the story of the Ten Commandments has Moses going up Mount Sinai to collect the two tablets. During his long absence, the Israelites fear that he might not be coming back, and instead ask Aaron to manufacture some idols for them. Aaron makes a large golden calf from the Israelites' melted earrings. When Moses returns, he is enraged by the idol, burns it, grinds it into powder, scatters the powder on water, and forces the Israelites to drink the water. He follows this up by ordering a killing spree. Most passages involving calves feature similar slaughter, as the animal's significance was largely sacrificial. Along with goats and lambs, calves were ritually slain. Following death, the carcass was often divided into two, and individuals who were making some form of agreement would walk between the halves as part of the ritual ratifying their covenant. It is believed that the implication of this Babylonian custom was that if either party reneged on the deal, they would suffer the same miserable fate as the dispatched creature. Calves were also sacrificed to appease for sins committed, although such an action was

Ancient Egyptians also worshipped calves, although their devotions were to the live animal itself.

Our relationship with the calf has been a complex one: while some peoples have deified calves, the modern desire for luxury leather goods and delicacies such as veal has roused animal rights activists.

> *It was not, in fact, young cows that were particularly held up as sacred by the early Hebrews, but the representations they fashioned had to be small due to the unaffordability of metal; therefore the images came to be known as calves.*

not considered to fully atone for the wrong that had been done.

The sacrificial calf also played a part in more convivial Biblical gatherings. Because it was considered superior meat, it was often offered up and enjoyed to give thanks for special fortune. It was common practice at the time to feed one animal a special, rich diet, which would keep it fat and enhance its flavor when it was finally killed and consumed. This would only happen in exceptional circumstances, illustrated in the New Testament parable of the Prodigal Son. Having wantonly wasted his inheritance abroad, a younger son hits upon hard times and returns home to his father's house. In joy at his son's return the father throws a huge celebration, and instructs his servants to kill the fatted calf—to the resentment of the elder son who had worked faithfully for his father all the while. The story is one of the best known from the New Testament, and the phrase "kill the fatted calf" now refers to a lavish celebration of a long-awaited homecoming.

The association of the fatted calf with the finest quality holds to this day. The high demand for breeding cows to satisfy market demand for milk results in a surplus of calves, whose only commercial use has been in the veal industry. While its enthusiasts praise the meat as a tender, low-fat delicacy, animal rights advocates

The high demand for breeding cows to satisfy market demand for milk results in a surplus of calves.

Ancient Indian texts compare the gods' devotion to their followers to a cow's dedication to her calves.

decry the methods used to prepare the calves, particularly the formula-fed ones who are kept in small crates that limit their movement to restrict the development of muscle fiber and maintain the tenderness of the flesh. This kind of veal farming has been banned in the United Kingdom, among other countries, and a concerted campaign is under way to get it outlawed in the United States as well.

While many of our relations with calves have an element of exploitation, the endearing creatures often capture the public imagination, and get people rooting for the animal to escape its typical destiny. During the height of Britain's hoof-and-mouth disease crisis in 2001, government officials visited a farm in Devon to kill its cows in accordance with regulations. Some 45 animals perished in the barn, but five days later when the officials returned to disinfect the rotting carcasses, one two-week-old calf—born, coincidentally on Friday the 13th—was

alive, mooing next to the body of her mother. Although she was certified as healthy, the officials insisted the calf had to be killed due to an outbreak of hoof-and-mouth disease on a neighboring farm. But when officials arrived to seal her fate, the farmer refused to allow it. Meanwhile, the case had been picked up by the press, who were running a campaign to rescue the calf, named Phoenix for her incredible escape, with celebrities and politicians adding their voices to the cause. The government eventually changed tack, and Phoenix was reprieved. She was subsequently retired from farm duty, and was adopted by the farmer and his family as a pet.

Deer

A baby deer's safety depends on it remaining undetectable by hunters, such as coyotes, black bears —and humans.

Deer are instinctively shy creatures. The phrase "like a deer caught in the headlights" accurately captures its paralyzing fear of confrontation. This is not an animal that typically seeks out human contact, its fawn even less so. And yet the fawn is familiar to generation after generation of children, having provoked an emotional connection and empathy that survive long into adulthood. The reason? Walt Disney. His 1942 animated film *Bambi*, based on an Austrian novel, follows a young fawn's journey from infancy to adulthood and his own fatherhood. The tale is etched in the memories of children the world over. Its themes, the loss of innocence and the cycle of life, are universal and the film has been translated into numerous languages. The scene where Bambi's mother is shot by poachers— even though this is not seen on screen—is held up as one of the scariest moments in American movie history by film buffs.

Forever the subject of fairytales, and the embodiment of grace and beauty, the deer, and its infant fawn, has captured the imagination of young and old for generations.

Camouflage is one of the fawn's major survival strategies, particularly on its mother's hunting forays, which can last several hours at a time.

This includes director Steven Spielberg, who described *Bambi* as the biggest tearjerker of all time, and said that seeing the movie as a child prompted him to get out of bed in the middle of the night to check that his parents were still alive.

Bambi may be the most famous fictional fawn, but he is not the only one. Four years before the movie was released, American author Marjorie Kinnan Rawlings penned *The Yearling*, which went onto claim a Pulitzer Prize the following year, and was made into a film starring Gregory Peck. The story follows a young boy who adopts an orphaned fawn called Flag. Like *Bambi*, the tale deals with the loss of innocence on the journey from childhood to adulthood and the harsh realities of life, survival, and death.

A doe cannot recognize the call of her young, but will remember where she left them and their scent. Once a fawn passes the "scent test", she will suckle it.

Over 65 years since *Bambi* and *The Yearling*, humankind remains one of the greatest threats to deer and fawns: humans have been hunting deer since 7000 BC. But while viewers of *Bambi* may recoil in horror at the prospect, North American hunters argue that the dense deer population makes such controls necessary. Deer cause thousands of road accidents, and scores of deaths, every year, usually as a result of overpopulation. They are particularly active at night, in an unfortunate conjunction with restricted driver vision.

Deer do not seek out such collisions. Indeed, from a young age they shy away from most kinds of confrontation. Aside from humans, coyotes and black bears also pursue vulnerable deer, and none are so vulnerable as the fawn, which has limited

movement for the first few weeks of its life. Fawns are usually spring-born animals, coming into the world in May or June, weighing between four and eight pounds (1.8 to 3.6 kg). Their reddish-brown coats are dotted with white spots, which they will lose before winter. When her young are born, after a gestation period that can last up to ten months, depending on the species, the doe's first priority is to lick them. This has no benefit in terms of nurturing or bonding—it is purely a self-defense mechanism. By licking, the mother is removing almost all traces of smell from her newborn. It must be undetectable if it is going to survive its mother's absence when she goes off to forage for food for several hours at a time. Does typically have small litters of two (occasionally three or four) fawns, so it is vital that they are protected, and the mother will go to extreme lengths to make sure they are. Although fawns can stand within an hour of their birth and walk short distances on their first day, they will not develop enough mobility to allow them to accompany their mother when she leaves, and must remain hidden. Young fawns hate the thought of being parted from mom, and often try to follow her. But the doe cannot allow her still-clumsy babies to slow her down. She must exercise tough love,

and sometimes has to physically keep a fawn in its hiding place by tenderly pushing it down with her foot.

The doe will choose a place protected by dense vegetation, where her offspring should be safely hidden. If she has more than one, they will stay separately. Their coats help: the fawn's reddish-brown hue and white spots serve as camouflage in the forest, and it must lie flat and still in its mother's absence. It must also refrain

from passing water or solids, as this can alert potential predators to its presence. Only when the doe returns is the fawn allowed to urinate and defecate, and in a display of impressive maternal devotion, the doe will ingest the result to remove all evidence of her fawn's existence.

A fawn can face danger from the most well-meaning source: people who come across lone young deer awaiting their mother's return often wrongly assume they have been abandoned and take them to be hand-reared—greatly depleting their chances of survival.

The doe will choose a well hidden site to secrete her young, protected by dense vegetation. If she has more than one fawn, she will leave them in separate places—the noise and movement of more than one together would alert predators.

Predators are not the only threat. In places where humans and deer share an environment, there have been cases of people happening upon a lone fawn. Assuming it has been abandoned by its mother, they remove it from its hiding place and take it to be hand-reared. Often, the mother is nearby at the time, but prevented from returning to claim her fawn by the presence of the very humans trying to help. Hand-reared fawns do not enjoy high prospects of survival when they are returned to the wild, and the gesture, though well-intentioned, spells disaster for both doe and fawn.

By studying the behavior of the mother and her offspring, biologists noticed an interesting quirk in the system. While the sequestered fawn is easily able to recognize its mother's sound, the doe cannot reciprocate: She cannot tell her own fawn's call apart from others of the species. To locate her young, she returns to the approximate place where she left them, and calls. Their mother's sound is the signal that it is safe to come out, and the fawns will then reveal themselves. To make absolutely sure that the approaching fawn is her own, the doe will perform a final check: the sniff test. Satisfied that maternity has been proven, she will then suckle her young. Her inability to distinguish her own young by their sound underlines the danger of humans removing a lone fawn: Its location is the only way by which the mother can quickly locate her baby.

After a couple of weeks, or perhaps a month, the fawn's spindly legs will have developed sufficiently to allow it to accompany its mother on her foraging trips. Grass and plants normally suffice for the herbivore deer, although there are reports that it will sometimes eat meat if it is desperate. Throughout its life, the doe will be the only parent a fawn knows: Unlike in *Bambi*, the father plays no part in its upbringing; the basic social unit is a doe and her fawns. While deer are, to a great extent, solitary animals, the bonds formed between the females can be strong and enduring. In some species, such as white-tailed deer, the male fawns will leave their mother at the end of a year, whereas the females may stick around for double that time. This is despite the fact that they reach sexual maturity at an early age—males typically at around two years, but females as young as seven months. And while the male fawn's goodbye to his mother will be final, females may return to their mother once they have had fawns of their own, to form close-knit herds. Female solidarity can even extend beyond family borders, with does sometimes grazing together in groups of over a hundred.

Deer are instinctively shy animals, with the phrase "like a deer in the headlights" accurately capturing the paralyzing fear they feel when faced with danger. They avoid all contact with other animals, including humans, whose vehicles can prove lethal.

Dogs

The bond between man and dog is greater than any other found in the animal kingdom, a bond that has existed for centuries. There is no better example of unconditional love and loyalty than that given by a puppy to its owner.

"Buy a pup and your money will buy love unflinching," wrote Rudyard Kipling in his poem *The Power of the Dog*. And puppies are certainly famed for their devotion, which often overrides any instinct of self-preservation. A dog's unceasing loyalty to a cruel owner is one of the most heart-rending aspects of our relations with "man's best friend." While, conventional wisdom has it, a kitten's attentions can be won away by the appearance of a saucer of milk from a stranger, a puppy will remain loyal to its owner until the end. This quality has made an imprint on our phraseology and culture: to follow someone

Puppies are famed for their love and loyalty, but a dog requires human kindness in its early days if it is going to grow up to be a good family pet. Training should be more like a game than a serious process.

Domestic dogs are descended from wild canines, and the traits that they shared with dingoes and wolves—neither of whom rate highly for family-friendliness—have not disappeared entirely.

around like a puppy dog means to love someone unflinchingly, as Kipling put it. Puppy love is a way to describe the kind of indiscriminate infatuation felt by teenagers, more in love with the idea of being in love than with the other person. It is referenced both in the Paul Anka song *Puppy Love*, later recorded by Donny Osmond, and in Elvis Presley's *A Dog's Life*. But while puppies are inextricably linked with such images of eagerness and cuteness, their sweet nature is not a given. Domestic dogs are descended from wild canines,

and the traits that they shared with dingoes and wolves—neither of whom rate highly for family-friendliness—have not disappeared entirely. Without socialization with humans at a young age, a puppy can become aggressive and vicious. Like their human counterparts, young dogs need tenderness, which is why experts recommend that the training of puppies should be more like a game than anything else, gentle and fun.

Once a puppy is well trained and socialized, it can improve human life immeasurably.

"Puppies are nature's remedy for feeling unloved, plus numerous other ailments of life," said dog enthusiast Richard Allan Palm. American author Sara Paretsky agrees: "When you feel lousy, puppy therapy is indicated." But puppies' usefulness goes far beyond their ability to lift our spirits and make us able to face the world again. For some people, puppies are an essential means for them to participate in society, take on their demon, or have any semblance of a normal life. The most obvious examples are guide dogs. The practice of using canines to assist non-sighted people was started in Germany during around 1916 by a German doctor, Gerhard Stalling, who began to train German Shepherds to guide soldiers who had been blinded fighting in World War I. Over a decade later, an American trainer of dogs for the police and army named Dorothy Eustis wrote an article about the movement, and was subsequently contacted by Morris Frank, a blind American. Mrs. Eustis arranged for a dog to be trained for him, and went on to set up a center in Vevey, Switzerland, which she called L'Oeil qui Voit, or The Seeing Eye, which inspired the organization of the same name. From the United States, the concept spread to Europe, after Mrs. Eustis sent one of her trainers to the United Kingdom at the behest of two British women in 1930. Although the project started with German Shepherds, today Golden Retrievers and Labradors typically perform the role. Training starts very young. Aptitude for the task comes from a mixture of breeding, conditioning, training, and affection. At the age of seven or eight weeks,

"Buy a pup and your money will buy love unflinching," wrote Rudyard Kipling in his poem **The Power of the Dog.**

pups will go and live with volunteer families, who expose their young apprentices to a variety of social situations with which they will have to cope once in service. At 18 months, their time with the host families is over, and the dogs move out to undergo several months of tuition and a final exam and then spend a further few weeks learning the ropes with their new owners before they are ready to go it alone. Assistance dogs are not limited to helping the blind. Some pups train as hearing dogs, alerting their owners to sounds from an alarm clock, doorbell, or kitchen timer

Puppies' usefulness goes far beyond their ability to lift our spirits and make us able to face the world again.

The British Guide Dogs for the Blind Association is the world's largest breeder and trainer of assistance dogs.

The puppy's wholesome and endearing looks have established it as a star of posters and TV shows, not to mention one of the best-loved and longest-running advertising campaigns in the world, for Kimberly-Clark toilet tissue.

to a smoke or other emergency alarm. Others help disabled people with opening doors, dressing, and shopping. The British Guide Dogs for the Blind Association, today the world's largest breeder and trainer of assistance dogs, estimates that around 75 percent of pups complete their training and end up in service with a visually impaired person. The rest may go on to become hearing dogs, assist disabled people, or join the police. Others are adopted by families as pets.

But the puppies who become the valuable eyes, ears, or hands for someone in need do not start their useful life upon moving in with their new owner. The pups' training process provides a unique opportunity to engage some of the more alienated members of the community, teaching them the life skills that they lack. The United States has pioneered programs that pair dogs with appropriate individuals, to the benefit of both parties. One group that has gained significantly through such programs is troubled high school students. The thinking behind the plan was that even disruptive and very shy youngsters liked dogs, and training puppies could be a way to get them to engage in something and learn the skills—such as patience, commitment, reinforcing positive behavior, and consistency—that were lacking in the kids' own lives. Proponents declared the project a success: school attendance went up by over 70 percent and students' self-esteem also rose considerably. The idea was subsequently adopted abroad. And schools were not the only institutions to see their members benefit from training puppies to become service dogs. In the 1990s, Florida veterinarian Dr. Thomas Lane hit upon the idea of getting prisoners involved in raising puppies and founded the first guide dog prison program. Not only did inmates have plenty of time to devote to caring for the puppies—which requires a lot of effort—but, as with the high-school problem kids, doing so would teach them important skills for their re-integration, such as taking responsibility for someone else, patience, giving and receiving unconditional

The puppy's charms must indeed be great if they can get through both to hardened criminals and troubled teens.

love, and teamwork. Gloria Gilbert Stoga quit her job as a member of New York Mayor Rudolph Giuliani's Youth Empowerment Services Commission to found Puppies Behind Bars in 1997, which took pups into prison for inmates to train as guide dogs. The animals have several weekends a month out of prison living with families, to become used to the things to which they are not exposed in prison, such as doorbells, car rides, and sidewalks, but aside from these sojourns, they spend all their time with their trainer. Inside the jail the pups are also used to encourage female inmates to open up and talk and to calm them down before attending parole board meetings. Prisoners, officials, and the disabled people who go on to receive the trained-up pups have all praised the program.

The puppy's charms must indeed be great

if they can get through both to hardened criminals and troubled teens. And it is these same charms that have made puppies among the most popular pets in the media, with books, films, and advertising campaigns all drawing on the puppy's appeal to get their point across. Numerous stories for children have used puppies to introduce their young readers to themes of innocence, responsibility, and growing up. The classic puppy tale must be animated 1961 Disney film *One Hundred and One Dalmatians*, based on the 1956 novel by English author Dodie Smith. The Disney feature was the highest-grossing movie of the year. In 1996 it was re-made as a live action feature starring Glenn Close as Cruella De Vil, who wants to kidnap the puppies for their fur. Her horrific intention of butchering the dogs in the name of fashion means that Cruella is often voted one of Disney's scariest villains. Other screen pups have also taken center stage. Great Dane Scrappy-Doo was introduced into the classic Hanna-Barbera cartoon *Scooby-Doo*, about a dog and his human friends who solved mysteries, in 1979, in an attempt to boost flagging ratings. Scrappy, Scooby's nephew, was in many ways an archetypal puppy: energetic, bold, and optimistic. Whereas Scooby was more inclined to leave

There is something in puppies' behavior that people seem to find endlessly entertaining—to such an extent that a television channel has been pioneered that consists of nothing but the antics of adorable pups playing around.

At the height of his popularity, canine star Rin Tin Tin was receiving 10,000 fan letters a week.

any potentially perilous dealings with monsters to the others in favor of getting some food, Scrappy was always spoiling for a fight, with his catchphrase "Puppy power!" But this cartoon pup was not deemed to share the endearing traits of his real-life counterparts. Viewers found Scrappy annoying, and his introduction was later judged to be proof that the series had run out of steam.

Other screen puppies have managed to accrue a larger fanbase. At the height of his popularity, canine TV star Rin Tin Tin was receiving 10,000 fan letters a week and was considered one of Hollywood's top stars. The original animal was French, discovered during World War I by Corporal Lee Duncan among the debris at a bombed-out war kennel with its mother, a German Shepherd, and siblings—the only survivors of the attacks. The pups were just five days old. The dogs were divided among

Puppy dogs eyes—the beseeching look as demonstrated by the black Labrador—are one of the animal's most endearing features, and a surefire means for a pup to get its own way.

the battalion, with Duncan taking two himself, which he named Rin Tin Tin and Nanette after puppets that French children gave the American soldiers for luck. Inspired by the performing German war dogs he had seen, Duncan trained his two pups up, even visiting the master of the bombed kennel to further his understanding of German Shepherds. Sadly, Nanette was taken ill on Duncan's return boat trip to the United States after the war and died shortly afterward, but the other pup survived, and the soldier, who had gone back to working in a hardware store, took Rin Tin Tin to various dog shows, where its jumping skills were captured by a photographer, whose film was then sold on to a studio. Duncan enjoyed the experience and tried to get his protégé back on the screen, eventually persuading a film crew to give him a chance to replace a difficult wolf with Rin Tin Tin in a scene they were having trouble with. The scene was shot in one take. The studio was Warner Brothers. Rin Tin Tin went onto make 26 movies for the studio throughout his lifetime, and is credited with saving the studio's fortunes. Duncan continued to be involved in dog training, including for the World War II effort, with Rin Tin Tin's heirs. A $1 million biography of the dog was reportedly commissioned in 2004.

It seems that our appetite for watching puppies frolicking is boundless. While watching the OJ Simpson trial in 1994, former advertising executive Dan FitzSimons found himself channel surfing during the slower parts of the proceedings. Frustrated with the surfeit of game shows, soaps, and reruns, he found himself wishing for a "filler" cable channel, something diverting to have on for a few minutes while waiting for another program to start. Who better to perform this function than puppies? In 1997, The Puppy Channel was launched, showing nothing but puppies playing around to a backdrop of soothing music. FitzSimons's daughter said that in focus groups, 41 percent of participants said they would

In 1997, The Puppy Channel was launched, showing nothing but puppies playing around to a backdrop of soothing music.

The Puppy Bowl, shown on Animal Planet, is a light-hearted take-off of the Super Bowl, and features puppies playing in a model stadium.

rather watch The Puppy Channel than CNBC, and 37 percent rated it above TBS. A year after its launch, it was included in four local networks. Although not currently going out on television, the promoters are pursuing the idea over the internet. Inspired by the same idea—that puppies at play are tremendously cute and watchable—is the Puppy Bowl. Shown on Animal Planet, the three-hour show is a light-hearted take-off of the Super Bowl, and features puppies playing in a model stadium. The show reportedly has the highest viewing figures of any cable show at that time. There's also a benevolent side: The participating pups have all been rescued from shelters, and the program broadcasts information about how viewers can adopt an animal or help their local shelter.

Advertisers have not been slow to capitalize on puppies' appeal. The so-called "Andrex" or "Cottonelle" puppy, the Golden Labrador that promotes Kimberly-Clark toilet tissue, became the first brand icon to be immortalized in Madame Tussaud's waxwork museum in London. The dog—at nearly four decades old, possibly one of the world's oldest "puppies"—graces packaging and ads in over 30 countries across North America, Latin America, Europe, and the Asia-Pacific region. Officials at the company have put the campaign's enduring success down to

So-called mongrels can be as endearing as pure breeds: The pup pictured above, looking bemused by the thick carpet of autumn leaves, nearly as high as he is, is a Bichon and Maltese mix.

The most high-profile pet puppies have made it all the way to the White House. John F. Kennedy, Bill Clinton, and George Bush Sr. have all welcomed puppies into the presidential fold.

the puppy's "emotional appeal that transcends language and nationality." The pup was premiered in the United Kingdom, where it has been voted the nation's favorite fictional TV character. It is estimated that one in ten British homes has the animal in a soft toy version. Puppy love has even infiltrated the ranks of the celebrity, with many of today's young female stars being inseparable from their tiny dogs. The public's dual fascination with famous people and puppies have been catered for in shows like Celebrity Dog School, which went out in the United Kingdom and Australia, where participants trained their pups and dogs for various tasks. But the most high-profile pet puppies have made it all the way to the White House. John F. Kennedy, Bill Clinton, and George Bush Sr. have all welcomed puppies into the presidential fold. Abraham Lincoln's famous pup, Fido, born around 1855, was another venerated pet, who followed his master around Springfield, Illinois, with a newspaper in his mouth. When Lincoln decided that Fido would be unsettled by the move to Washington, and left him in the care of a local family who had previously befriended him, he left a horsehair sofa that Fido had enjoyed sleeping on, and instructions that the dog was to be indulged rather than scolded.

But despite the near-universal love of puppies, from President to pop star to prisoner, the animals

As well as playing vital roles in the rehabilitation and mobility of groups as diverse as the blind, disaffected teenagers, and prisoners, puppies generally boost human spirits, as summed up by author Sara Paretsky: "When you feel lousy, puppy therapy is indicated."

still suffer at the hands of humans, even though cruelty to canines is associated with wickedness and lunacy, as summed up in the English proverb, "He that would hang his dog gives out first that he is mad." The demand for pups as pets has resulted in puppy mills, some of which have been criticized for the poor conditions in which the dogs are kept. The poor standard of food, lack of space and healthcare, unsanitary conditions, and lack of socialization are some of the charges leveled at the mills. Even when a pup reaches a home, its potential troubles are not over. Seduced by a puppy's cuteness, many families overlook the commitment and work that goes into caring for a young dog, and choose to abandon their animals. This is particularly common after Christmas, when a puppy who is given as a gift soon finds its novelty is wearing off. The mass post-holiday abandonment led the British association The Dogs Trust to run a campaign to persuade people not to buy puppies unless they had seriously considered the effort required and could commit to looking after the dog. The slogan "A dog is for life, not just for Christmas" was coined in 1978, and is still in use today.

For the majority of households, though, the arrival of a puppy heralds joy, comfort, fun—it has even been found to boost children's health. This is in part due to the effects of exposure of

infection on the immune system, but the pleasure from owning a pup cannot hurt either. Charles M. Schulz, creator of Snoopy, one of the world's most famous dogs, sums it up best: "Happiness is a warm puppy."

Dolphins

Dolphins have long been regarded as a highly intelligent species, which have come to the aid of seafarers many times. Their young must learn survival skills from their mothers from the moment they are born.

Popular wisdom has it that dolphins are the one species whose intelligence comes close to our own. Our respect for their cleverness combined with countless stories of pods of dolphins saving swimmers from shark attacks have combined to form a strong bond between human and dolphin, celebrated in fictional characters such as Flipper, whose astuteness and helpfulness cast the creature in the role of a marine Lassie.

But despite their famed intelligence, dolphins do not sail easily through life. At birth, a calf has just a 50 percent chance of survival, with sharks and humans—despite our high regard for the species—their main foes. The first challenge is to be able to breathe properly. Calves are born beneath the surface of the sea, usually tail first, after a gestation period of about a year. But being mammals—not fish, a common misconception—they cannot breathe underwater. After labor, which typically takes around half an hour, the mother will gently nudge her newborn up to the surface of the water, where it will take its first gulp of sea air. Sometimes this requires prompting. If the baby cannot figure out how to use its blowhole and breathe on its own immediately, the mother will softly tap its stomach, throat, and chest until it does. The calf will in almost all cases be alone, as dolphin twins are very rare, and there are no known instances of twins surviving. At this stage the baby measures about 2.5 to 3 feet (75 to 90 cm), and weighs between 30 and 90 pounds (14 to 41 kg).

Nursing presents similar logistical challenges to birth. While both mother and calf hold their breath, the baby clamps its snout tightly to its mother's nipple to feed. She is able to speed things up by ejecting milk into her offspring's hungry

Unlike with other species, the mother does not see off her young to devote all her attention to the next arrival; a young calf will stick around, until anywhere from three and six years old.

mouth—enabling the pair to quickly reach the surface for air. In time, both will become experts. While young dolphins start to feed on fish from a few months old, they continue to benefit from their mothers' rich milk for up to two years. Unlike with other species, the mother does not see off her young to devote all her attention to the next arrival; a young calf will stick around even following the birth of a sibling, until anywhere from three and six years old. During their time together, the mother must impart survival skills, such as catching fish, squid, and crustaceans, as well as self-defense. More basic skills, such as swimming, the calf masters instinctively. By this time young females are themselves reaching sexual maturity, with their brothers not far behind. Even after they go their separate ways, dolphins retain their family ties. Throughout their lives they stay in defined home ranges, and family reunions are not uncommon.

This social support network is a key aspect of survival. Dolphins do not form lasting bonds with their mates, and do not practice fidelity, but the mother is not left to raise her young alone. Even as early as labor, an "aunt" or "midwife" dolphin—although not necessarily a female—stands guard, warding off the attentions of sharks and overly interested others.

Sticking closely to its mother is an important safety strategy for a baby dolphin, who—despite the creature's renowned intelligence—faces disheartening survival odds of 50:50 when it is born, with the main dangers being sharks and humans.

The natural affinity of dolphins for midwifery has so impressed humans that the creatures have even been drafted into "assisting" with some human births.

The social network is a vital part of dolphin life right from the off, when an "auntie" or "midwife" dolphin will assist the mother giving birth, and then stick around for the first few weeks to ensure the new mother and baby get off to a good start.

The helper will protect the new mother and baby for weeks. Their natural affinity for midwifery has so impressed humans that the creatures have even been drafted into "assisting" with some human births.

First-time dolphin mothers certainly need all the support they can get. Maternal skills are a vital factor in a baby's chance of survival, and these improve with every pregnancy and child, so firstborns are at a distinct disadvantage compared to their subsequent siblings. Establishing a strong mother-child bond is essential. To that end, as soon as a calf is born, the mother will begin to whistle to it persistently. This has two advantages: one, the baby will recognize its mother's sound in the event of a separation. The second objective is to encourage the calf to develop its own whistle. Such safeguards against separation are indispensable, because the sea can be a dangerous place. The number-one enemy is the shark, some breeds of which prey on dolphins. And the

animals also continue to be victims of the tuna fishing-industry, despite huge public pressure on fishermen to change their methods and the advent of dolphin-friendly tuna. Schools of tuna commonly swim below dolphin pods, which made dolphins a magnet for the fishermen hunting the tuna. Using the old methods, dolphins were frequently killed or injured being caught up in the nets, but scientists were baffled when the new techniques did not result in improving dolphin populations. Ironically, it appeared that one of the creature's most efficient and labor-saving habits was also its undoing. A calf moves by sticking close to its mother, staying in her slipstream—the suction created by a moving object. But the system works only when the pair are in close proximity. Startled by approaching tuna fishing boats, female dolphins instinctively speed up. The calf may then be left behind, resulting in permanent separation. Without its mother's milk and protection, its survival chances

As soon as a calf is born, the mother will begin to whistle to it persistently. This has two advantages: one, the baby will recognize its mother's sound in the event of a separation. The second objective is to encourage the calf to develop its own whistle.

plummet. Such divisions are not always the result of human intervention. It is believed that childless female dolphins use the technique to kidnap babies, swimming quickly past a mother and calf and dragging the baby with her in her own slipstream.

There is little that we can do to intervene in this kind of calf snatching. But campaigns are being waged across continents against the human practices that deplete the dolphin population, in some cases potentially threatening eventual extinction. There have been some successes, with laws banning the more deleterious kinds of fishing coming into force. Such small but important victories go some way to boost the survival odds of one of the world's most respected, altruistic, and intelligent creatures above a mere 50-50.

Donkeys

The donkey shares a long history with humanity, from biblical times to the present day. Always dependable, the donkey has always enabled mankind to complete tasks that it would not have been able to accomplish alone.

The humble donkey is one of the species most put upon by humankind. Despite featuring in one of Christianity's most glorious moments—Christ's triumphant return to Jerusalem on Palm Sunday—it is more commonly associated with burdensome work, stubbornness, a low station in life, and miserable longevity. With its long ears and braying voice, donkeys are often depicted in film and literature as somewhat dopey figures of fun, such as the gloomy Eeyore created by the British author A.A. Milne for his *Winnie-the-Pooh* stories. This is an impression which has stuck, and few people realize that donkeys' comical features were essential survival tools in a harsh environment, and that the animals are in fact highly intelligent, loyal, and gentle, and can often make wonderful pets.

Wild asses, from whom today's donkeys are descended, developed after the last Ice Age, in North Africa, the Middle East and Southern Europe. Less forceful than some of their equine relatives, they ended up in the more barren areas shunned by other animals, mainly hills and deserts. Adapting to their inhospitable living conditions, they developed coarse, wooly coats, which were necessary to protect them from extremes of both hot and cold. They became unfussy with regards to diet, surviving off whatever could be found, however ostensibly meager. A donkey will eat grass, bark, leaves, herbage, thistles, and shrubs—much of which a horse would turn its nose up at.

The typical gestation period lasts just under a year, but 14 months is not unheard of. The duration of the pregnancy depends on many factors. The mother's age, her past births, the sex of her foal, and any infection can all influence precisely when a foal comes into the world, as

"Poor little Foal of an oppressed race! I love the languid patience of thy face;" wrote Samuel Taylor Coleridge in a 1794 poem about a foal that grazed the grass at his university, which the poet befriended.

can the region and even the weather. Most foals are born singly, although there are rare instances of twins. Although the success rate of twins is relatively low, it is still far higher than for horses. Like humans, during pregnancy a jenny (the name for a female donkey) needs a stress-free atmosphere for her newborn to prosper. She needs exercise and can undertake light duties until the last quarter of her term. When the birth is imminent, the mother may seek solitude or become slightly hostile to other animals. The foal will appear feet first, with its nose, resting on top, poking out soon after. Within half an hour the birth is over. Barring any complications, the jenny is perfectly able to manage the delivery unaided. Her first maternal task is to lick her foal dry, both to stop it from becoming chilled—the donkey's coat is great protection against cold and heat, less so against water—and to kindle her mothering instinct, which is particularly important in the case of first-timers. Jennies may not naturally take to motherhood, and some even resist nursing. Occasionally donkey breeders have to step in and encourage the female: this nourishing first milk, or colostrum, which the newborn foal should start feeding on in its first half hour of life, is essential for its wellbeing and vitality. A donkey's milk is said to be the closest alternative to human milk. It has even been touted as the secret to longevity, as a favorite tipple of María Esther de Capovilla, an Ecuadorian matriarch who was the world's oldest person at 116 when she passed away in 2006. It has been cited as having anti-aging properties and treating whooping cough,

although claims it can help in the fight against AIDS, cancer, and tuberculosis remain unproven.

Although the foal is on its feet within an hour—an impressive achievement compared with our own newborns' pace of progress—it is more vulnerable than appearances suggest. Its dense, fluffy fur may look protective, but for the first two weeks the animal needs shelter from the elements. Too early exposure to rain can get the foal chilled, and put it at risk of a potentially fatal dose of pneumonia or bronchitis. Nursing continues for around six months, although the foal may take its first nibbles at its mother's food within two to four weeks. The baby learns from its mother, and a premature separation, before around six months, can be emotionally damaging.

A donkey's milk is said to be the closest alternative to human milk. It has even been touted as the secret to longevity, as a favorite tipple of María Esther de Capovilla, an Ecuadorian matriarch who was the world's oldest person at 116 when she passed away.

Its dense fluffy fur may look protective— but for the first two weeks it needs shelter from the elements.

"That which is called firmness in a king is called obstinacy in a donkey."

John Erskine

Although some Jennies are not naturally maternal and have to be encouraged, young donkeys learn survival skills from all of their herd.

| *Donkeys are easy-going and amiable creatures, eschewing the territorial and hierarchical behavior of their horse cousins for a more egalitarian system.*

In their early days together, the presence of a male donkey, or jack, is bothersome for the mother. However, she becomes fertile again very soon after the birth, and the foal may be joined by a sibling after 14 months or so. It is quite common for a jenny to produce 15 foals over the course of her life, which could be as long as 40-50 years.

As the foal grows, it develops typical donkey characteristics. Its predecessors' rugged environment ruled out flight as an option in times of danger, so the donkey learned to use its wits to outsmart a foe instead. One technique it adapted was freezing to avoid doing anything under duress. This has been interpreted as stubbornness, giving rise to the popular simile, "as stubborn as a mule." In fact, the donkey is just buying itself some thinking time. An intelligent animal, it does not take kindly to overt displays of anger, which can greatly reduce the chances of winning the donkey's cooperation. In contrast, when living among their own, they are easy-going and amiable creatures, eschewing the territorial and hierarchical behavior of their horse cousins for a more egalitarian system. In this herd atmosphere, the foal learns survival skills and life lessons from its mother as well as the other members.

The geniality of the classless herd makes a stark juxtaposition to the cruel treatment that donkeys and foals receive from man. The animal's placid nature and carrying ability have made it the ideal beast of burden, and its reluctance to retaliate mean that it bears brutality stoically. A foal's painful passage through life is the subject of a classic French art movie, Robert Bresson's *Au Hasard Balthazar*. From Balthazar's idyllic foalhood days with loving children, he passes through a succession of uncaring owners, bearing all his suffering with dignity. As film reviewer Vittorio J. Carli wrote, "If any film can convince the audience that animals deserve rights, this is it." Bresson's work is often infused with religious symbolism and Balthazar, who also dies on a hillside, has been interpreted as a representation of Christ. The animal's association with Jesus is not a modern one—foals also make significant Biblical appearances. The most famous is Christ's return to Jerusalem on Palm Sunday, which he makes upon a foal. The story imparts an important Christian tenet: humility. The Book of Matthew describes onlookers saying, "Look, your king is coming to you, humble, and mounted on a donkey, and on a colt, the foal of a donkey."

This idea of donkeys and foals as being low, humble creatures persists throughout various cultures. While the donkey's cousin, the horse, has been celebrated, and put to such exalted uses as carrying soldiers into battle and racing at royal events, the donkey has been restricted to menial tasks such as beach rides and carrying packs. American author John Erskine wrote, "That which is called firmness in a king is called obstinacy in a donkey." And the image of a donkey as fixed in its lowliness is echoed in the Turkish proverb, "A worthy man is still worthy even penniless; a donkey is a donkey even if he is finely saddled."

But others have taken a more benevolent view. In India, where the tough conditions for many people perhaps make them more prone

Despite its reputation for stubbornness and stupidity, the donkey is an intelligent and calm animal and makes a gentle pet; its placid temperament makes it a popular choice for riding programs for handicapped children.

"To carry his loads without resting, not to be bothered by heat or cold, and always be content: these three things we can learn from a donkey,"

A herd animal, the foal learns much of its behavior from its fellow donkeys, who, unlike their horse cousins, eschew territorial and hierarchical behavior for a more egalitarian and peaceable social system.

to empathy, the donkey is held up as an example of diligence. "To carry his loads without resting, not to be bothered by heat or cold, and always be content: these three things we can learn from a donkey," goes an old proverb. And in the United States, similar associations have elevated the donkey, which is the established political symbol, albeit never officially adopted, of the Democratic Party, whose members cite the animal's courage, love, humility, and intelligence as its salient characteristics. Foals in particular have also inspired artists. The English Romantic poet Samuel Taylor Coleridge wrote the 1794 poem *"To a Young Ass"* about a foal that grazed the grass at his university, Jesus College in Cambridge, which the poet befriended and would feed and pet. *"Poor little Foal of an oppressed race! I love the languid patience of thy face;"* opens the work. It goes on to discuss the foal's pitiable plight, and

Coleridge speculates that if life treated it more equitably, the young foal would frolic like a lamb or kitten, rather than hang its head.

Doubtless many of today's foal and donkey enthusiasts would agree. The animals, after appropriate selection and training, participate in riding programs for handicapped children, to which their size and gentle temperament are well suited. The famed donkey patience also leads many families to choose foals as pets, with jennies or gelded jacks being the best options.

It seems that despite their humble reputation, the animals retain their devotees and empathizers. Coleridge sums it up best:

"I hail thee Brother—spite of the fool's scorn!"

Ducks

The duck is officially the world's funniest animal. As part of a year-long study of humor around the world in 2002, British psychologists and academics concluded that, of all creatures, it is the duck that engenders the most laughs and silliness. As the lead psychologist, Professor Richard Wiseman, summed up, "If you're going to tell a joke involving an animal, make it a duck."

Perhaps it has something to do with the bird's ungainliness. By no means the avian world's most proficient flyer, the duck also lacks the swan's grace and power. Cultural representations of the bird have often been in the form of comical, even hapless, cartoon characters. Its prosaic qualities have also led to the bird being used in the so-called "duck test" to rebut philosophical arguments about the nature of appearance and reality. Originally, the test was coined in 1950 by the United States Ambassador to Guatemala, Richard Cunningham Patterson Jr., as an analogy to illustrate that his host country's government

Ducks and ducklings are perennial children's favorites; their characteristics have been copied in cartoons and children's fairy stories alike. Ducklings especially, embody the clumsy and awkward values of youth as they grow into full grown ducks.

The duckling has been portrayed in culture and folklore as a somewhat hapless creature, an underdog with whom children can empathize, most notably in the classic fairy tale by the Danish author Hans Christian Andersen, The Ugly Ducking.

> *Baby ducks, of course, have the element of cuteness to add to their appeal in stories, parables, and analogies, and as such have become a favorite creature in children's stories.*

In some places, nine out of ten nests are destroyed by predators. Baby ducks are at particular risk in their early weeks as they are unable to fly. This exposure gave rise to the idiom "a sitting duck."

at the time was a Communist-style one, despite not describing itself so. Patterson put it thus: "Suppose you see a bird walking around in a farmyard. This bird has no label that says 'duck.' But the bird certainly looks like a duck. Also, he goes to the pond and you notice that he swims like a duck. Then he opens his beak and quacks like a duck. Well, by this time you have probably reached the conclusion that the bird is a duck, whether he's wearing a label or not."

Baby ducks, of course, have the additional element of cuteness to add to their appeal in stories, parables, and analogies, and as such have become a favorite creature in children's stories, often used as a kind of underdog with whom young readers will empathize. The most famous such story is *The Ugly Ducking*, a classic fairy tale by the Danish author Hans Christian Andersen. Among a mother duck's brood is one duckling who stands out for his grayness, large size, and clumsiness. Despite his mother's attempts to accept him, he is hounded by the other ducks and driven out of the family. On his own, and with nobody to accept and love him, he nearly

perishes over the course of the winter. Finally, he comes upon a group of swans, and is struck by their beauty. Although he expects them to be as cruel to him as everyone else has, to his surprise they welcome him into the fold. When he catches sight of his reflection, he sees that, in fact, he too is a swan. The tale gives hope to victims of bullies, low achievers, and outsiders everywhere, that whatever rejection and difficulties they are experiencing, the future may bring success and acceptance. The term "ugly duckling" has entered common parlance to mean a person who blooms late after an unpromising start. On another level, the tale also suggests that moral

goodness will win out over physical appearance. *The Ugly Duckling* touches something universal in the human psyche—our need for the love and approval of others—and has been subject to numerous retellings in literature and on screen.

Other literary ducklings have also captured readers' hearts around the world. When American writer and illustrator Robert McCloskey returned to Boston, Massachusetts, a few years after his scholarship at the Vesper George Art School, he saw a family of ducks negotiating the traffic near Charles Street. The image stayed with him. His 1941 book *Make Way for Ducklings*, is about the adventures of a family of eight baby ducks

trying to find a home in Boston. To perfect his illustrations, McCloskey studied at the American Museum of Natural History in New York, before eventually adopting six ducklings who moved into his studio to work as models. His endeavors paid off: the book won the 1942 Caldecott Medal, a prestigious prize for illustrators. But the ducklings left a more tangible legacy. A statue of them by the local sculptor Nancy Schön was erected in the Boston Public Garden, the park where the animals live in the story. It seems that ducklings have a charm that transcends linguistic and cultural boundaries. In testament to the story's international success, a replica 40-foot

The classic image of ducklings, swimming along in a line behind their mother, as above, is a result of imprinting, the process by which baby ducks follow the first moving object they see. It also helps to keep them safe from predators.

Feeding the ducks in the local park is often among young children's early experiences of interacting with the natural world.

(12 m) statue was built in Novodevichy Park in Moscow in the early 1990s, a gift from then First Lady Barbara Bush to her Russian counterpart Raisa Gorbachev and the children of her country. Meanwhile, in the United States, Boston has hosted a Duckling Day Parade every year since 1978. The event sees children get dressed up in baby duck costumes, as they and their parents retrace the path from the Charles River to the Public Garden taken by the ducklings' mother, Mrs. Mallard, in the story. A similar duck parade—although in this case with real birds—takes place twice daily at Memphis's famous Peabody Hotel, when the birds march on a red carpet through the hotel lobby. Their human-friendly temperament, as opposed to their more aggressive cousins, swans and geese, make duck families ideal for human association, with feeding the ducks in the local park often among young children's early experiences of interacting with the natural world.

Ducks are social creatures and like to congregate. For this reason, anyone who does not have a lot of time to give a pet duckling is advised to buy more than one. The one time a mallard, or mother duck, will seek solitude is when she's about to give birth. However, ducks trust each other's judgment, and anywhere another duck has chosen to lay eggs will seem a good bet to a mallard. Duck breeders can mimic this technique using a golf ball. Often, a duck's breeding ground will be where she herself was hatched. While still on the scene—male ducks are not attentive fathers following conception—the drake will protect the breeding ground, seeing off other couples who try to move in. Meanwhile, the female will set about building her nest. Ideally, it should be above water, to give the ducklings a soft landing on their debut outing, but close to water will suffice. After she lays her eggs—between half a dozen and a dozen is normal—she may sit on them to keep them warm and safe, although some breeds are broodier than others. The typical incubation period is 28 days, during which time the developing duckling must be regularly turned by its mother. It breathes through the 7,000 pores in its egg, and feeds off the nutritious yolk, thanks to which, the newborn

Baby ducks are at particular risk, not only from their fragility and naivety, but because for the first few weeks of life—between five and eight—they are unable to fly.

duck needs neither food nor water for its first 72 hours of life. The duckling heralds its intention to enter the world with a gentle tap and its first noises. As Bill Ivy describes it in his book, *Mallard Ducks*, "A tiny 'peep peep' comes from one of the eggs. Her long wait is over—her eggs are about to hatch. After a few minutes a small hole appears in the noisy egg... then a crack. Finally the shell splits in two and out steps a brown and yellow duckling with its feathers sticking up in wet spikes. Weak from the effort of breaking out of the shell, it sits quite still and looks around bewildered." Ducklings are born fluffy and adorable, making them the darlings of art prints and cute calendars. Baby ducks are quickly able to move around, and leave the nest for the water on their second day, led by mother.

The classic representation of ducklings is in a line, swimming along merrily behind the mallard.

Behind this image is the scientific process of imprinting. Instead of recognizing their mother in particular, imprinting leads ducklings to form an attachment to the first moving thing they see, friend or foe. In the event that it is foe, the duckling is done for. Mostly its first contact will be with its mother, but baby ducks have become attached to human beings and other friendly animals, and started to follow them. Austrian naturalist Konrad Lorenz did much of the pioneering work on imprinting, winning a Nobel Prize in 1973. It was he who discovered that a duckling will socially bond with even an inanimate object, such as a white ball. The imprinting instinct, when operating successfully, is instrumental in the important life lessons—what to eat, whom to fear, and where to hide. It also keeps the ducklings close to their mother, meaning she has a chance of defending her young if an enemy strikes. They are

A mallard usually gives birth to between half a dozen and a dozen baby ducklings, often at the same place where she herself was hatched; meanwhile the drake protects the breeding ground, seeing off other couples who fancy moving into the territory.

Some mallards are less resistant to outsiders and will even adopt ducklings whose mother has abandoned them or died.

vulnerable to a plethora of creatures—raccoons, foxes, mink, turtles, large fish, snakes, plus large birds such as herons, hawks, eagles, and peregrine falcons. In some places, up to nine out of ten nests are destroyed by predators. Baby ducks are at particular risk, not only from their fragility and naivety, but because for the first few weeks of life—between five and eight—they are unable to fly. This exposure gave rise to the idiom "a sitting duck," meaning an easy target. By contrast, once it can take to the air, only humans and peregrine falcons present any real danger. But predators do not always come in the most obvious form. Ducks sometimes kill their own. A drake may slay ducklings to

encourage the mallard to mate again, while a female may also slaughter an interloping baby. Some mallards, however, are less resistant to outsiders and will even adopt ducklings whose mother has abandoned them or died.

Despite our fondness for ducklings, and our adoption of them in our stories, posters, and hearts, humans remain one of the chief threats to their wellbeing. While both duck and duckling meat are shifting from delicacy to mainstream food, humankind's reckless use of the world's resources and resulting contribution to climate change is also throwing the duck world off kilter and jeopardizing the survival chances of baby ducks. Like baby chicks and lambs, ducklings are

typically born in spring. But fluctuating climatic conditions, such as unseasonably warm winters, have skewed the creatures' typical cycles and resulted in ducklings being born even before Christmas. This leaves them vulnerable to sudden cold snaps. When ducklings are cold, they huddle together for warmth. But even this form of cooperation, one of their key survival skills, is of limited use in an increasingly unpredictable environment.

Elephants

The majestic elephant is the largest land animal in existence and it is known for its maternal characteristics. Herds are made up of mothers, aunties and daughters who vigorously protect their young against predators.

Wisdom, memory, and intelligence are three of the qualities with which the elephant is often credited. And the creature has long been a friend to humankind, using its colossal strength to assist us in our endeavors for some 5,000 years. It is also one of the animals whose life cycle most closely resembles our own. With a life expectancy that can reach around 70 years, a period of female fertility from the early teens to the late forties, and even a kind of menopause plus the onset of age-related diseases, the human journey has many parallels with the elephantine one. So there is one aspect of our own culture shared by the elephant to

With a gestation period of up to 22 months, the bond between the baby elephant and its mother is one of the strongest in the animal kingdom, and infants will stay with their mother for years, daughters sometimes indefinitely.

which we can fully relate and empathize: the overwhelming bond between mother and child. The arrival of a new baby is celebrated joyously by the whole community in the elephant kingdom, as in our own. If anything, a female elephant invests even more than her human equivalent in her calf, with a pregnancy twice as long as a woman must endure. Her young will stay with her for years, learning the skills that are essential for their survival, her daughters perhaps indefinitely. It is no surprise, then, that we can understand and identify with the strong maternal attachment that is at the heart of the elephant's endurance. What is surprising is that in so many parts of the world, human behavior is responsible for rending that bond in two, to the detriment of mother, child, and the entire elephant population, which is now teetering on the brink of extinction.

Even without man's harmful intervention, the odds are stacked against the elephant from the very beginning, with high infant mortality rates, sometimes as much as a third or even a half. Elephants in captivity face an even tougher challenge. Maternal instinct and mothering techniques are mostly learned from the herd, by watching other mothers give birth and raise their young. Deprived of that, an animal in captivity can often make little sense of what is happening to her, and reacts to the emergence of a small elephant from her belly with shock rather than love. In some cases the mother can refuse to nurse her newborn, something that breeders and zookeepers have to fight hard to persuade her to do, as deprived of its mother's nutritious milk a calf's health prognosis is not good.

A female's first pregnancy typically happens around the age of 13. She will have chosen the biggest, strongest, and oldest mate possible for the purpose. A mammal of excess in many ways, the elephant's gestation period is another record—the longest of any land mammal, at between 18 and 22 months. Given the epic length of her pregnancy, it is little wonder that around three to five years will typically pass before she feels inclined to go through the whole process again. Labor, too, can be dauntingly protracted, lasting from anywhere between five minutes and 60 hours; around 11 hours is typical.

Maternal instinct and mothering techniques are mostly learned from the herd, by watching other mothers give birth and raise their young.

It is a risky procedure. Elephants prefer to stand to give birth, meaning the newborn literally tumbles into the world. If it falls badly, injury and even death may result. This is where the animals' cooperative ethic comes into play. An assisting "midwife" elephant, known as an allomother, is on standby, ready to soften the baby's fall to earth with her trunk. Her next duty will be to break the amniotic membrane if it does not break on its own.

The calf is typically born weighing around 250 pounds (113 kg) and three feet tall. This is just four percent of its eventual weight if female, and two percent if male. Its sight is not well developed at this point, and it will be reliant on touch, smell, and sound to identify and recognize its mother. Job number one is to clear its nasal passage of fluids, to which end it will sneeze or snort. The next challenge is to get to its feet, which is essential if the calf is going to nurse; this is accomplished with mom's help. Within between half an hour and one hour it will take its first wobbly steps, often leaning against its

The calf is typically born weighing around 250 pounds (113 kg) and three feet tall. This is just four percent of its eventual weight if female, and two percent if male.

Maternal behavior is learned by the herd, which means that elephants kept in isolation in captivity can have difficulty in relating to their newborns, sometimes even initially refusing to nurse their young, which greatly damages their survival chances.

mother's legs for support. Its mobility develops fast. Within a few days it will be able to keep up with a slow-moving herd, and at three months old is capable of moving around entirely independently. A high degree of independence is also required when nursing, which the calf must also do unaided. It has a lot of growing to do, putting on from 2 to 2.5 pounds (0.9 to 1.1 kg) a day, and to this end requires a staggering 24 pints (11.3 liters) of milk a day. Its reliance on its mother's milk as a sole nutritional source diminishes from around the age of three months, when it will begin to sample an adult elephant diet, which typically consists of grass, leaves, fruit, foliage, roots, branches, and twigs. But the calf will continue to nurse for anything up to five years or longer, or until the arrival of a sibling. But even this does not always terminate the nursing period—in many cases a newborn and older calf will nurse concurrently.

The fact that a second baby does not steal away all the mother's attention is another example of the elephant's sophisticated social support system. From the moment a newborn comes into the world, its welfare is the business of the whole herd. The main social unit is the matriarchal herd, which consists of related adult females, presided over by the eldest, as well as young of both sexes. The group provides a vital network of support, information, and practical help, with other animals joining the original allomother in assisting the new mom. It is also responsible for teaching the calf what it needs to know. A newborn elephant's brain is between 30 and 40 percent of its eventual adult size, and there is a lot of learning to be done. Very little of a baby elephant's skill set is programmed innately. The calf, as much as its mother, must learn from what it sees. One reason why the valiant attempts to rear calves in captivity are so often futile is because the wealth of knowledge that comes from the herd is absent. Initially, for example, the calf's use of its trunk is comically clumsy. It will wave it around in wonder and trip over it. Only through seeing other animals pick things up, scratch, drink, and so on will it start to copy and gradually master the use of its unique appendage. One adult use for the trunk—administering corporal punishment to wayward babies—will not impress it quite as much.

But the highly developed learning system that is so crucial to baby elephants' wellbeing and even survival is coming under increasing pressure from humankind. With their impressive stature and intelligence, it seems that elephants, of all animals, would be relatively robust

A baby elephant has a lot of growing to do, and puts on from 2 to 2.5 pounds (0.9 to 1.1 kg) a day with the help of a staggering 24 pints of milk (11.3 liters). It may nurse for as long as five years, and even the arrival of a sibling does not necessarily put an end to its suckling.

Elephants' size and strength deter most predators from the natural world—except, in some cases, lions.

creatures, able to see off the majority of threats to their species. Quite the opposite is the case. While elephants' size and strength deter most predators from the natural world—except, in some cases, lions—damaging practices like the trade in ivory and big game hunting have all depleted elephant populations. Their huge size, so often an asset, works against them in hunting, where speed and the ability to hide are the essential advantages. The animal is now listed as endangered by the World Conservation Union, and restrictions are in place on the treatment of elephants and trade in ivory. But poaching and hunting persist. Poachers are most drawn to the larger elephants, because their tusks

From the moment a newborn comes into the world, its welfare is the business of the whole herd.

yield more ivory, meaning that the herds are deprived of their adults, their chief source of protection and education. The outlawing in some places of logging, which employed many animals in heavy lifting work, has driven the practice underground, where conditions for the creatures are even worse: they are prodded with spears and even fed amphetamines to make them work faster. Some former logging animals are now used on the streets to beg for money. There is little incentive to take care of these elephants: Many owners even believe that a stricken animal is likely to elicit more money from sympathetic passers-by.

Part of the problem is the sheer weight of human numbers. The animals live predominantly in Africa and Asia, both of which are seeing growth spurts in the human population. As people take over more of the land for their settlements and industry, elephants are finding their own environments significantly reduced. Nor are they creatures that can easily manage in a small space. The volume of food required—a massive 300 to 500 pounds (137 to 227 kg) per day—must be sourced from a large area. In this area, too, hunting works against the elephant.

As other large game are picked off, the smaller grazing animals who would typically fall prey to bigger predators can multiply, providing more competition for the elephant's already scarce sources of nourishment. This, along with their ever-shrinking environments, pushes the animals reluctantly into closer proximity with humans. The resulting crop raids and rogue elephants—males who become aggressive in their breeding season—set human and animal against each other, and deaths can occur on both sides.

The consequence of all of this, plus the difficulties in raising elephants in captivity, is that at the present rate of decline, some biologists expect the species to be extinct by 2010. The animal that author Rudyard Kipling called "a gentleman" and the 17th-century English poet John Donne described as "nature's great masterpiece, the only harmless great thing" may be relatively harmless itself, but the harm inflicted upon it looks likely to make the baby elephant's great battle for survival one that it may ultimately lose.

Elephants are highly social animals: a newborn is considered the business of the whole herd, with the other females in the matriarchal group helping the allomother out in assisting the new mother as she gets to grips with parenthood.

Geese

Geese are hardy animals that can be vicious when protecting their young. Because of this characteristic they have been used in place of guard dogs in farming communities; often being more defensive than any dog could be.

Baby geese are fortunate enough to benefit from one of the tightest family set-ups in the avian category. Their parents mate for life, and their fathers stick around to protect and raise their offspring—something of a rarity in the natural world, which seems populated by single-parent families. With geese, though, it really is a case of "until death us do part." Goslings are in no rush to flee the nest, staying with their parents for a year or two, and not venturing too far from them after that. Home remains where the heart is, and geese return to the same nesting and feeding areas year after year—even if they must fly 2,000 or 3,000 miles (3200 to 4800 km) to do so.

The monogamous parents usually meet in the winter, either on their migratory routes or wintering grounds. They breed just once a year, in March and April in the United States. While the female is laying her eggs, the male stands

Geese are among the few animals lucky enough to enjoy the attentions of both parents throughout their infancy, and later return to the same nesting and feeding areas year after year, regardless of the distance.

guard nearby, but not close enough to lead any potential predators to the scene. The average clutch of eggs laid in one session is between two and eight. The creamy white eggs incubate over 25 to 28 days, with the mother goose regularly turning them to maintain the right temperature. When it is ready to come out, the baby uses its egg tooth, a small protuberance on its beak, to break through its shell, a process that can be time-consuming, lasting a whole day. The newborn goslings are covered with soft down. Their eyes are open—and the fascinating process of imprinting begins, by which the newborn goslings bond emotionally with the first moving object they happen to see. Usually this is the mother, but a gosling can also form a strong attachment to a human if the association is made early enough, after which it will accept food by hand, follow its owner around, and submit to gentle petting. A young goose imprinted on its owner will even favor human company to that of its peers.

Generally, though, imprinting works as nature intended, cementing a strong familial bond that will last a lifetime. The day after the clutch finishes hatching, the newborn goslings are mobile enough to leave the nest. Typically, given the devotion and commitment of their parents, this is a family affair. Goslings, gander, and geese vacate the nest en masse, traveling together, feeding, and looking for appropriate shelter. Parenting duties are shared, with both

the mother and father feeding and guarding their newborns. And it is when on guarding duty that geese, not generally known for their viciousness, can become suddenly aggressive if they sense that their family is in danger. The goslings' first six or seven weeks are their most vulnerable, as they have not yet developed one of their most important survival skills: flight. Geese nests attract skunks, foxes, pet dogs, raccoons, some turtles, and birds such as ravens, crows, and gulls. To defend their young, geese have devised a well-practiced system. The male sounds the alarm, simultaneously flying upwards and making a honking noise to warn not only his family, but others nesting in the area. Hearing the alert, the female spreads herself over the nest, stretching out her neck to provide her chicks

with camouflage. In the event that they need to fight, both male and female will give it their all.

A creature's desire to save its own offspring is an understandable evolutionary impulse. But geese's parenting goes beyond the basic urge to pass on genes. Lone birds or same-sex pairs will often raise orphaned goslings with the same devotion as a natural parent. Such admirable familial tendencies have led to the birds being adopted as symbols of marital loyalty and happiness. Baby geese were commonly given as a wedding gift in Central Europe, and also featured in marriage celebrations in China and Korea.

Guinea Pigs

The Guinea Pig is a popular domestic pet. They owe their appearance in Europe to the exploration of the 'New World', and rapidly became kept by Queen and commoner alike.

Synonymous with the subject of an experiment, the Guinea pig is remarkable firstly for its misleading name: it is neither from Guinea, nor a pig. A gentle animal, rarely given to aggression, it is a common sight in school classrooms, where it provides many a child's early introduction into the miracle of life and responsibilities of caring for another living being. The species is one of the more popular members of the rodent family, having none of the insalubrious associations of rats and mice. But like its rodent cousins, the Guinea pig is a ferocious breeder. A female animal bought from the pet shop will typically be pregnant already, and, within a few short weeks of their birth, Guinea piglets can themselves become fertile, often with chaotic and sad consequences for unprepared owners. From birth, a passage of time not even as long as the gestation must pass again before the baby animals reach sexual maturity. To put this into a human context, it is the equivalent of a baby

being able to reproduce at something like six months old.

Despite being entirely unconnected with the porcine world, Guinea pigs share a lot of its terminology: females are called sows, males are known as boars, and the young are Guinea piglets, or sometimes pups. The species as a whole is sometimes referred to as cavies, from the Latin name, *Cavia porcellus*. In the United States and Europe, the creature is known solely as a fairly ordinary pet, with little in the way of extraordinary talents. In South America, by contrast, not only do the animals roam in the wild, they also play a significant part in the local culture. Given as presents on special occasions such as weddings, to guests and to children, they were also routinely used in Andean medicine, when the animal was rubbed over a sick patient. It was believed that when it began to squeak, the source of the malady could be identified as the area just below its position. Rare black Guinea pigs were considered especially holy. It was Dutch and English traders who first brought the animal from South America to Europe at the start of the 18th century. Its popularity as a pet owes much to one of the early owners, Queen Elizabeth I of England. From there, enthusiasm for the Guinea pig filtered down via the aristocracy to the general public.

Doubtless the ease of keeping cavies, their friendliness, and their hardiness also lie behind the animal's popularity. If cared for properly

Though a fairly ordinary family or classroom pet in the United States and Europe, in parts of South America the Guinea pig was traditionally thought to have diagnostical powers, and was commonly used in medicine.

In the United States and Europe, the creature is known solely as a fairly ordinary pet. In South America, not only do the animals roam in the wild, they also play a significant part in the local culture.

they have few health problems and seldom bite or scratch. The main problem they present to owners is with their high fertility. Sows typically reach maturity at between six weeks and three months, but it is not unknown for a female to conceive as young as three weeks old. While sows are in heat for approximately one day only out of 18 or so, boars are able to mate all the time, and will pester and try to mount any females—sometime even males—in the vicinity. If a female is not in heat or simply not interested, she will run away, snap, and bite at him, or—as a last resort—expel a small jet of urine in his face, which is usually enough to get the message across. If, however, she is interested in mating, she will respond to his advances, and the pair will copulate several times an hour, often with only

a few minutes' break in between, to ensure a successful conception. In pregnancy, sows need double their usual amount of food, and swell to a shape resembling an eggplant.

After a gestation period of around 60 to 70 days, the female will give birth to a litter of around five pups. If the litter is larger, the gestation period is generally reduced. Although these prolific breeders often cope well with pregnancy, the timing is key. Labor too early in life, when the sow is still young herself, often means that she is too small for a successful delivery, and is also likely to lack the maturity necessary to raise her young charges. Old age presents another set of problems. From around ten months of age, if she has not previously given birth, a sow's pelvic bones fuse, restricting movement and inhibiting labor. This is especially problematic because baby Guinea pigs are born in a very well-developed state, and the sow's pelvic bones must separate enough to create a gap of just under one inch. Without this, a Caesarian section may be necessary and the birth will be difficult—often fatal—for both mother and offspring. Between five and nine or ten months is the ideal time for the first litter, and if she conceives in this period, future litters are likely to be free of complications, and the sow can hope to have another three to four over the course of the next four years. Guinea pig boars are involved fathers and usually play a part in raising their offspring. However, towards the end of her term, a mother may find her imminent brood's father an annoyance, and owners can ensure a less stressful late term and delivery by removing him from the cage. In any case, unless he has been neutered, he should definitely be

removed following the birth. Within an hour, the sow is fertile again and a second pregnancy so soon would be a huge physical burden for her to bear. As well as disruptive fathers, pregnant sows should also be separated from each other. One going into labor can induce the process in another and bring on premature delivery, even if both were impregnated at the same time. Guinea pig sows also require a peaceful pregnancy, as any stress can result in miscarriage, premature labor, and stillbirth.

Labor typically lasts around half an hour, with each pup taking about five minutes to emerge,

In pregnancy, sows need double their usual amount of food, and swell to a shape resembling an eggplant.

at a weight of three or four ounces (85 to 113 g). The mother's first job is to bite through the sac that envelopes each baby in her womb. Failure to do so will result in suffocation. Next, she licks her babies clean, with help from the father if he is still present, then brings her young to a safe and warm corner of the hutch where they will cluster around their mother. Feeding is not an immediate priority: newborns are born with enough nourishment to last them for their first 24 hours. Unlike many other mammals, they are not reliant on colostrum from their mother for immunization. Baby cavies are precocial—relatively mature and mobile from the moment of birth. Their eyes and ears are open, they have their full complement of hair and teeth, and within a few hours they are happily running around and exploring their new environment. Although they are capable of eating solids within a few days, the pups will suckle for two or three weeks, which helps them to grow faster. However, the nursing process is not as vital as for some other mammals, and the piglets are quite capable of surviving without it. Nor is nursing strictly between mother and baby—other females who are still lactating may well share feeding duties.

Baby cavies are relatively mature and mobile from the moment of birth. Their eyes and ears are open, and they have their full complement of hair and teeth.

Guinea piglets' social bonds are formed early in life, so human contact in the early days are an important step in socialization. This makes no difference to the mother's acceptance of and love for her young. During the nursing period, babies stick closely to their mother and father. One manifestation of this is the Guinea pig train, one parent leading and the other bringing up the rear, with the babies forming a line in between, ensuring that nobody gets lost. If a baby does become separated from the family, it will squeak loudly until brought back into the fold. Alas, the family paradise is short-lived. Once the piglets are weaned, they will already be approaching sexual maturity, and the males and females must be separated to prevent inbreeding.

Their furious appetite for procreation was depicted in *"Pigs is Pigs,"* a famous short story by Ellis Parker Butler that was published in *The American Magazine* over a century ago, and made into a Disney cartoon in 1954. It tells the story of a railway agent who tries to charge collection of a shipment of two Guinea pigs at the higher rate for livestock, rather than the lower domestic animal fee, based on his misunderstanding of their name, which he interprets as implying they are pigs from Guinea. While the argument rumbles on and the relevant bureaucracy is navigated, the animals begin to mate in the station house. The outcome is that the agent decides to charge the lower rate for all livestock in the future.

Ellis Parker Butler may have found an amusing angle on their prolific breeding, but in reality it is one of the chief causes of Guinea pig welfare issues. Even well-intentioned home breeders may be overwhelmed by the demands of such numerous litters, and can be unprepared for delivery and labor complications. Animal shelters are full of abandoned Guinea piglets, and they urge would-be breeders to give a place in their home to one of these rather than bring more into the world. Animal rights activists warn that the cavies seen in pet stores can end up as snake or reptile food, or even bait for dog fights. Guinea pigs might not have the fear of extinction hanging over them, but that does not mean that their life is a picnic.

Dutch and English traders first brought the Guinea pig from South America to Europe at the beginning of the 18th century. One of the early adopters was Queen Elizabeth I of England, whose pet cavy popularized the animal among the British aristocracy.

Horses hold a special place in our lives and history. They have been an integral part of man's world since the dawn of civilization and we have put them to use for purposes as diverse as farming and warfare.

Horses

Expectant women waiting at home for days on end for the arrival of their child, or those whose newborn decides to make its way into the world mid-flight, or in a remote location, may envy the horse for one of its abilities: namely, to decide on the precise moment of labor, delaying it for hours or even days until a time of the mother's choosing. In this way the animal thwarts any humans who are keen to witness the spectacle. The birthing mare prefers her solitude, and she will do her best to make sure she gets it.

An expectant horse can postpone labor for hours or even days, and pause mid-birth, to ensure she gets the solitude she craves for the delivery. For this reason, many foals are born in the middle of the night.

Despite humankind's close relationship to the animal, there remains some confusion about the baby horse. A pony is not, as many people assume, a baby horse, but one of several breeds of horses that conform to certain criteria of temperament and size. The term has since been extended to cover any small horse. A baby equine, however, is called a foal, with a male known as a colt and a female a filly.

The lives of horses differ tremendously whether they are wild or domesticated. Several horse species resisted human domestication.

All but one are now extinct, and that one is on the endangered species list. But even domestic horses still retain their herd instincts, watching other animals, particularly the herd leader, for clues as to how to behave, and recognizing that their main weapon against predators is speed. Whether wild or tame, the animal's entrance into the world is much the same. The baby emerges after a gestation period of around 11 months, during which the mare is said to be "in foal." Twins are rare, occurring around once in every 10,000 births, according to biologists. Some vets consider that the horse's physical makeup does not permit her to bear twins, and that when they are conceived, one will typically die during the pregnancy and be re-absorbed by the mare. The majority of foals are born at night; estimates suggest that between 75 and 85 percent of horse births take place between 6pm and 6am. This seems to be the way by which the horse gets the privacy and security she wants for the delivery. Not only can the mare postpone labor if she is being checked up on, she can also halt the proceedings midway if an unwelcome observer happens along, and continue after their departure, exercising an impressive degree of control over herself. As well as the spike in nighttime deliveries, spring also sees a larger proportion of foals being born, with the annual peak between April 15 and May 15.

Signs of an imminent birth differ significantly from one animal to another. While some mares will cease eating, start pacing restlessly, and getting up and down to shift the foal into the correct position, others will simply lie down and get on with it. Labor, for which the horse lies

down, is not especially protracted, taking between 15 minutes and an hour. Immediately afterward, the mare will treat herself to ten minutes of rest, while her newborn starts to take in its new environment. The umbilical cord breaks either at this time or when the foal first stands up, which is about an hour from birth. This first attempt to get to its feet is naturally a clumsy and tentative procedure. From a sitting position, the baby horse will muster all its effort to stand—often trying too hard and projecting itself into a head-over-heels movement that deposits the eager animal back on the ground again. Undeterred, it attempts the mission again and again, until it successfully manages to remain upright. The first period of standing will be quickly terminated by a fall, but the foal perseveres, standing each time for slightly longer while its confidence builds. Even at this time, the newborn is well developed, weighing about 100 pounds (45 kg). It can already see, and will have cut its teeth within a week. Like other precocial animals, a baby horse is capable of movement at a very early stage. In fact, its legs are already 90 percent of the length

they will eventually be when the animal reaches adulthood, hence their slightly disproportionate, spindly aspect at the beginning. The newborn foal can follow the mare around as early as 20 minutes after birth, and within a couple of hours, it is walking, trotting, even running. Within a day, a wild foal is able to keep up with the herd. However, despite its impressive mobility skills, in the first few days it seldom ventures too far from the protection of its mother, to whom it will show an instinctive affinity. This bond is not always immediately reciprocated. A mare foaling for the

The first period of standing will be quickly terminated by a fall, but the foal perseveres, standing each time for slightly longer while its confidence builds.

first time may respond with alarm to the small replica that has just emerged from inside her. She may even attempt to bite or kick her offspring— and the kick of an alarmed horse is not something to which a vulnerable young animal wishes to be exposed. At this stage, some human intervention is appropriate with domestic horses, and the mare should be controlled while the approaching foal makes first contact. With this, her fear usually subsides, and the bonding process can begin.

It is vital that this contact is not too significantly delayed, as there is a certain window when the foal is at the peak of its receptivity to information and influences. Imprinting may be more associated with ducks and geese, but it is also an important technique for rearing young

A mare foaling for the first time may respond with alarm to the small replica that has just emerged from inside her.

foals. Something that a baby horse can absorb in minutes, shortly after birth, could take much more time and effort to impart when the foal is older. People who wish to ensure their animals are comfortable around humans should take this opportunity to pet the foal and subject it to all the things that it may be exposed to later—taking its temperature, putting on its halter, making loud noises. If this happens early enough—even while the foal is still lying down—and is repeated throughout the first 24 hours, the animal will be much more cooperative and comfortable when it goes through the same thing later in life. But like the baby duckling convinced that a white ball is its mother, the phenomenon—and the horse's general tendency, as a herd animal, to learn by copying others—can have some incongruous results. In 2007, British newspapers reported the case of Rory, an eight-week-old Shetland pony foal, who was behaving like a dog. Rejected by his mother, the foal was transferred to a horse sanctuary, where illness meant he spent much of his early life being cared for in the office. The stable owner's two dogs took an active interest in the foal, and the three animals spent a lot of time together, during which Rory learned to wag his tail, chase sticks, and roll on his back to have his tummy tickled.

Whether it is learning from dogs or the more conventional means of other horses, the foal is active and full of life, eager to explore its new environment. For this, it needs a plentiful supply of energy. The foal gets this from its mother's colostrum, a rich milk that will help provide the baby with immunity against disease until its body

can take over the job itself. If the foal expends too much energy by walking around before it has been fed, it will become weak. Nursing usually starts after about three hours, and there is a cut-off point of eight to twelve hours, after which the antibodies can no longer be absorbed. A weak foal may require this nourishment

At birth, a foal's legs are already 90 percent of the length they will be when the animal reaches adulthood.

Horses are herd animals and even the domestic breeds retain their herd instincts, looking to other animals, in particular the leader of the group, for indications of how to behave, what to eat, and—most importantly—how to stay safe.

Given adequate food and water, a lactating mare can produce up to three gallons (11 liters) of milk daily, which helps her offspring grow rapidly, putting on three pounds (1.4 kg) in weight a day.

Colts eventually become a threat to the main stallion and must leave the herd, although they are sometimes allowed to stay close by in a so-called "bachelor band." Fillies, meanwhile, come to the attention of other bachelors, and ultimately depart of their own volition.

via a stomach tube. Given adequate food and water, a lactating mare can produce up to three gallons (11 liters) of milk daily, which helps her offspring grow rapidly, putting on three pounds (1.4 kg) in weight a day. From ten days old, it will venture to try solids, often nibbling a little from its mother's feed, although nursing is still enough to meet its nutritional needs. By eight or ten weeks, however, it requires another food source. At the age of four to six months, it is time for the foal to be weaned. While the moment of release from this demanding maternal duty may be welcomed by the mare, her foals face it with trepidation. It is the first step on a nerve-wracking journey that, in the wild, eventually sees the foal leave the herd.

Throughout its youth, the foal has been nurtured and raised by the older horses. However, a colt eventually reaches an age and strength where he could be perceived as a threat to the lead stallion. Colts may be permitted to follow the main herd until they find another herd to join. In some cases, they join together to form what is known as a "bachelor band." The young horses will stay together until they are capable of taking on another lead stallion for supremacy, with the ultimate goal being to tempt away some mares

from other herds to form a new one of their own. Fillies depart the herd in a very different manner. As they approach sexual maturity, at around three years of age, they come to the attention of bachelors, and may opt to go off for a few days with a new suitor. Although these dalliances do not go far from the herd, the filly's relatives voice their displeasure. In some cases, this act of "disloyalty" results in the horse's permanent exclusion from her original herd. Other times, she will be accepted back into the fold, with her paramour remaining in the vicinity to continue their connection. Eventually, though, the filly will commit to a stallion and make her departure.

The horse's journey from carefree foal to beast of burden and then peaceful retirement is chronicled in the enduring 19th-century novel *Black Beauty*, by British author Anna Sewell. The pathos of the cruel treatment suffered by the horse has touched the hearts of generations of children, and the book now stands as one of the early calls for animal rights.

Lions

The king of the beasts has always captured the public imagination. These majestic creatures have many cubs, who are cared for by their mothers until six to eight months.

Although celebrated for its strength and dominance, lion populations are in dramatic decline, due in large part to human hunters and scarce food supplies. In some places lions are threatened with extinction, with cubs particularly vulnerable.

So-called "king of the jungle," the lion has long been a symbol of strength and supremacy. *Aesop's Fables* depicted the concept of the lion's share, in which the big cat was happy to benefit from the labors of lesser creatures—but kept all the spoils for itself. This bears some relation to real life. But this grand reputation obscures the truth about the lion: its population is declining at a dramatic rate, and in certain places some species of lion are on the endangered list. Cubs are particularly vulnerable.

What could be so deadly that it could harm the powerful lion? One answer, as ever, is humankind. Rich tourists travel to parts of Africa and pay top dollar to hunt lions. Their kills not only affect the particular animals shot, but their tendency to go to a bigger, more "prestigious" prey means that adult males are popular targets. With the primary male gone, there is no one to see off the male cubs when they reach sexual maturity, which results in damaging inbreeding between sons and mothers and sisters. Another factor in the falling lion population is lack of food. Although protective parents in many ways, lions will not sacrifice their own share of the provisions, and so when food supplies drop, the babies are the first to suffer. Cubs can even

A pride's females synchronize breeding, so all nursing and supervision can be shared, some animals on maternal detail while others are out hunting—a chore that falls predominantly to the lionesses.

meet their end from their fellow lions, intent on limiting the competition for scarce food or freeing a potential mate of her current maternal duties. The upshot is a high mortality rate, with only 20 percent of baby lions making it to their second birthday.

Vulnerability is a fact of life for lion cubs. They are born after a very short gestation period for an animal of the lion's size—around 108 days on average. After such a brief gestation, newborn cubs are blind—it will be around two weeks until they can see properly—and tiny, weighing in at just a pound (450 g). Seeking love and protection, they stay close to the adult females of their pride. Thanks to the small size of the litter, typically between one and four cubs, and the long period between pregnancies, the cubs have little competition for attention, and stay with their mothers for around two years. The lioness does not have far to look for babysitters. A pride's females synchronize breeding, so all nursing and supervision can be shared, some animals on maternal detail while others are out hunting—a chore that falls predominantly to the lionesses. Nursing continues for six or eight months, after which the cubs begin to spend more time with the hunters, learning to kill. But while they learn

vital survival skills from their mentor lions, the same animals are also potential threats. A lioness will, on occasions, see off her own cubs in the rush for food, and the males sometimes have to step in and ensure the young get enough nourishment. And yet male lions present an even greater danger. When the lead lion begins to ail, the pride is vulnerable to a takeover bid from a rival male or coalition, the group of mating males that accompanies the females. The time between the interloper amassing the strength to mount such a challenge and the point when his own star will wane is brief, so he must mate soon. The new head lion will therefore kill off any cubs, making sure the females are fertile and receptive to his advances. Although she will fight desperately to prevent the slaying, a lone lioness

is usually too weak to succeed. However, a few females in concert sometime manage to save the cubs.

Life in the pride is not always so brutal. Lions can rely on each other for protection and care when times are tough. Pride members have been observed bringing meat to wounded lions who would otherwise have faced starvation.

Lions can rely on each other for protection and care when times are tough. Pride members have been observed bringing meat to wounded lions who would otherwise have faced starvation.

Lions enjoy a solidarity that contrasts starkly with the solitary existence of the tiger. The females of a pride even synchronize breeding, so they can share babysitting and nursing duties between them.

Monkeys

Our closest relatives in the animal kingdom share many characteristics with us, especially in the way in which they care for their young. Monkeys and their babies have always fascinated humanity, due to both their physical similarities and their mental aptitude.

Monkeys' close connection to humans has been both a boon and a burden. While their sometimes uncanny similarity to us has won them the affection and devotion of many, it has also led to much cruelty being visited upon them, by separating them from their mothers and turning them into pets, and, of course, by the many scientific experiments performed upon them in the name of advancing human knowledge. Some of these tests look at the strong parent-and-child bond that most primates share. Like us, monkeys have a long gestation period. In most species, one baby is born at a time, and the mother will desist from having another for some time, in order to devote all her maternal energies to her one youngster. This dedication results in many baby monkeys enjoying high odds of making it through to adulthood. Deprived of its mother, however, a baby will suffer both mental and physical damage, while the anguished female can take months to emerge from the depression brought on by her loss.

Much monkey behavior closely resembles our own, particularly in the area of maternal devotion: female monkeys give birth to one baby at a time, and then spend the next few years putting all their energy into their infant.

The use of animals in such experiments presents a paradox. While, as the closest creature to humans, scientists argue that they offer the most accurate and relevant results, the same similarity makes us deeply uncomfortable about their suffering. Some of the most controversial tests were performed by Harry Harlow, an American psychologist. Harlow's experiments looked at the effects of separating a baby monkey from its mother and leaving the primates in isolation for as long as two years. In the maternal deprivation tests, he observed that the monkeys, desperately missing the maternal relationship, would bond with a substitute mother, a piece of cloth. The isolated baby monkeys became severely disturbed, leading to an outcry against the cruelty of the experiments, which many people believe helped kick start the animal liberation movement.

Public outcry at the trauma suffered by monkeys in scientific procedures has led to a drop in such experiments in some parts of the world, particularly in Europe, although the numbers used in the United States have remained fairly consistent over the last few decades. But baby monkeys are often separated from their mothers for other purposes. Their appeal—both as a result of their human-style behavior and the sweetness common to most baby animals—has made them popular as pets. To meet this demand, newborn monkeys are sourced both from captive animals, where they may be removed at anything between three days and a few weeks of age, and from the wild, where the mother is often killed to facilitate the capture of the baby. Even the "luckier" captive mothers who survive may spend months recovering from the ordeal of the enforced separation. And this is not the only risk for captive females. In the wild, monkeys learn much of their behavior, including maternal conduct, from the other members of their troop. Deprived of examples of motherly love and care, captive animals may reject and even harm their young. The babies who are sold as pets

Regardless of the species, though, the bond between mother and baby monkey is strong, with the young staying close to mom for several years.

seldom fare much better than their grieving mothers. Some die through inappropriate shipping methods. Robbed of its prized parent, the young animal suffers psychologically and physiologically. Its muscles do not develop properly, it may contract bone disease, and it is also likely to exhibit behavior similar to the actions of human children when they are deprived of the appropriate parental care: rocking, thumb-sucking, self-grasping, and even self-mutilation. And once it loses its baby-faced charm, and reaches the less agreeable state of sexual maturity, many families abandon their pets, which, ironically, are usually considered too "human" even to be placed in a zoo. Their fate may be in the laboratory.

There is some considerable variation from species to species. Gestation can last anywhere between five and nine months depending on the breed. Most female monkeys will give birth to just one baby at a time. A lot of investment goes into each infant, and the mother prefers not to have her attention divided. An exception is the Cebidae family, a group of New World monkeys, among whom twins are more common. Regardless of the species, though, the bond between mother and baby monkey is strong, with the young staying close to mom for several years. The father's involvement varies.

Monkeys' great similarity to humans has been both a boon and a burden for the animals: while we regard them with great affection, they have also been used in medical experiments that have greatly alarmed animal-rights activists.

In some species, such as the Marmoset, he will carry his offspring for the majority of the time, with the mother only taking over to fulfill her nursing duties—which often last until a sibling comes along. Among many other monkeys, the father considers his contribution completed at conception, and plays little part in bringing up his offspring.

Either way, with one active parent or two, raising a baby monkey is demanding. Newborns are not born with great mobility, and initially they must cling for dear life to their mothers or fathers. Later, when they develop enough strength to grip, they will typically be transferred from the front to the back, and ride along on top of the parent. When the animals are not on the move, the baby will usually be playing. However, like their human cousins, monkeys have distinctive personalities, and while some may be rambunctious, eager to mess around with their peers, others cling nervously to their moms.

Female monkeys can be fiercely protective of their young—but that it not to say that they do not share their duties and babies. Many monkeys have developed a sophisticated system of group parenting. Capuchins use a kind of mentoring process, whereby a young male or female shadows a mother and newborn, watching how the female cares for her baby.

Either way, with one active parent or two, raising a baby monkey is demanding. Newborns are not born with great mobility, and initially they must cling for dear life to their mothers or fathers.

At the end of this apprenticeship, which lasts around two and a half to three months, the young monkey is permitted to carry the baby and play a more active role in bringing it up and caring for it. The system benefits all three animals. The mother gets some much-needed downtime, allowing her to fraternize with the males of the troop, to ensure that her family will continue to grow. The younger monkey in the babysitter role learns the important parenting skills it will need in the future for its own young. And the baby gets to spend time with the younger troop animals, enjoying itself and gaining its own skill set: social behavior, foraging, and climbing. In some species, such as the spider monkey, new mothers will share the rearing duties—a phenomenon known as allomothering—in the absence of any input from the fathers. Males are discouraged from participating, as younger ones might inadvertently harm the babies. Throughout this, the mother remains in charge. But the troop's solidarity will be evident in an emergency: if a baby takes a fall, the monkeys will all pitch in to retrieve the stricken youngster.

But while tumbles may occur from time to time for young babies, they soon learn the necessary mechanics. Monkeys are fast learners and intelligent creatures. Their proverbial ability to produce the complete works of Shakespeare on typewriters if given long enough may be apocryphal, but they still have impressive communication and mathematical skills. Part of this is down to their early aptitude for imitation, previously thought to be limited to humans and chimpanzees. Researchers have noticed that in the short time following their birth, baby monkeys copy the facial movements made by both humans and adult monkeys. Scientists believe that this may help launch the face-to-face communication that helps the species flourish.

Paternal involvement in raising young monkeys varies from species to species. The mother and baby orangutan pictured here will go through life as a single-parent family, with the father playing no part in bringing up his offspring after conception.

Penguins

Clumsy on land and graceful in the water, penguins are often portrayed as comic characters and their young even more so. They survive in extremely cold temperatures and have evolved unique methods of protecting their young from the cold.

For all animals, from the smallest mouse to the largest elephant, by way of humans beings, labor and birth are somewhat trying. But whatever discomfort the typical mammal may endure, few would wish to swap with the penguin. Bringing a baby penguin into the world requires starvation, resulting in the loss of up to a third of body weight, an epic trek, and exposure to some of the most hostile weather conditions the planet can muster. After all of that endurance, the slightest misstep or lack of coordination, and the precious egg is irretrievably lost to the big freeze, rendering the massive effort futile.

If they are to thwart the extreme conditions and successfully raise a chick, teamwork is required. Typically, the female lays just one or two eggs, although in some species, such as the Adélie penguin, the female can have up to three. Given the cold weather, incubation is vital for the egg. In some breeds, the mother and father share the duty, taking shifts sitting on the eggs for several days at a stretch, while the other is away feeding—the conditions required for the breeding ground mean it is often far from water and the nearest source of food. In other species, this job falls to the father, who faces a cold and hungry wait that sees him weaken significantly as he waits for his mate to return, cradling the egg carefully on top of his feet. For some, all the efforts will have been in vain: up to a third of eggs can fail to hatch. From courting to hatching, an emperor penguin male will eat nothing, surviving on just his body fat. Incubation lasts up to two months, after which time the chick will tap a tiny hole in its egg. It chips away, making the gap bigger and bigger until it can nudge the top of the shell off. This is just the first of many big tasks for the penguin: it can take around three days to force its way out. When the chick does emerge, it is cold, vulnerable,

Few creatures go through the risk and discomfort of breeding borne by the penguin: epic treks, freezing temperatures, near starvation—on top of which, the slightest slip in holding the egg or newborn or transferring it between parents, and it could freeze to death.

In some breeds, the mother and father share the duty, taking shifts sitting on the eggs for several days at a stretch, while the other is away feeding—the conditions required for the breeding ground mean it is often far from water and the nearest source of food.

and hungry. With luck, its mother will be near with a vital supply of food to regurgitate and feed to her young. An emperor penguin father, even in his weakened state, may also be able to regurgitate some secretions. But unless the mother reaches them in time, the resources will not be sufficient, and the father may be forced to abandon his chick rather than perish himself on the long journey to eat.

Even if the mother does make it back safely and in time, the danger is not over. To free the male to go and feed, the parents have to transfer the newborn from the male's feet to the female's. This is a delicate operation, and as with the egg, if the chick is too exposed to the cold, it will freeze to death. The adult birds try to protect their newborn from the elements using their brood patch, a naked patch of skin around the abdomen that is thick with blood vessels. Baby penguins are also born with down to insulate them. But the down must be replaced with waterproof feathers before the chick can go into the water and find its own food. Until that point it remains entirely dependent on its parents.

| A king penguin chick must reach 13 months before it is prepared for its first swim.

Adélie chicks face a relatively short wait, of just seven weeks, while a king chick must reach 13 months before it is prepared for its first swim.

In the early days, the chick stays as close as it can to one or both parents. But some species also have another self-protective mechanism called a crèche. Here, young birds gather together while their parents are away seeking food. It is a case of safety in numbers, with the group protecting its members both against the cold and from predators. To reunite after periods of separation, parents and baby have learned each other's unique sound—penguins look as similar to each other as they do to us. Biologists originally thought that the crèche was a form of communal daycare for the chicks, with the adults all doing their bit to help the group. But the birds proved not to be quite so altruistic: each parent brings food only for its own chick. The other chicks are useful for warmth and self-defense, but nothing more. The one exception to this

rule, the one time a female will take an interest in the offspring of another bird, is following the loss of her own chick. A bereaved female will sometimes attempt to snatch another female's baby. However, such an endeavor rarely meets with success, as other females who witness the attempt will band together to help the real mother retain her infant.

The main danger, however, comes from outside the penguin community. Several creatures keep a keen eye out for a vulnerable or lone penguin chick, from the orca, or killer whale, to leopard seals, and even fellow birds such as giant petrels and Antarctic skuas. Ironically, birds of prey like the petrel ignore the corpses of the many chicks who did not make it to target live birds—the dead ones are too deeply frozen for consumption. Assuming that the chicks can avoid both freezing and their predators, they will grow in confidence, and start to spend increasing amounts of time away from their parents, returning only to feed. Eventually, some time between the ages of three and eight, the chick reaches sexual maturity, and the whole process begins again. The extraordinary journey of the emperor penguins was chronicled in the Oscar®-winning documentary *The March of the Penguins*.

Pigs

The pig is often derided as a dirty animal and comical character but the reality is far from this. They are actually very intelligent animals and are very caring of their young; the mother pig can suckle litters of up to fourteen babies.

Our view of pigs seems to contain several contradictions. Although the animal—and particularly its baby—is celebrated through our culture in the form of several much-loved characters, its name also stands as an all-purpose insult. Pigs are considered dirty—with "pigsty" serving as the standard comparison for a teenager's messy bedroom. But the animals are, by contrast, exceptionally clean-living. There is also an assumption that pigs are stupid, whereas they rank fourth for intelligence in the animal kingdom, outsmarted only by chimpanzees, dolphins, and elephants, and can often learn tricks quicker than dogs. A further falsehood is inherent in the phrase "sweat like a pig"—the animal is incapable of sweating. The other common pig simile, "eat like a pig" is also fallacious: it is water that is the most important part of a pig's diet. With its scrupulous hygienic standards, intelligence, and a complex and highly developed communication system, the animal is far from the lumpen livestock that it is unfairly maligned as being.

However, lifelong fidelity is not among the pig's qualities: male pigs, or boars, mate with several females in a season. There is one exception. The warthog, a wild pig that lives in Africa, sometimes mates for life. It is that continent that sees the most committed unions between pigs. African males stay with the group throughout the year, and participate in raising their young, while male warthogs depart after breeding, but later return to resume their paternal duties. Elsewhere the males and females mix only in breeding season, with the boars expressing their interest through chasing and vocalizing. The female—called a gilt if she has not bred before, and a sow if she has—stays with the boar for two or three months. Although she has a monthly cycle of being on heat, it is the presence of the boar that brings on ovulation.

Three months, three weeks, and three days after conception, the litter is due. The image of the sow with a row of piglets feeding from her is an iconic one. The 19th-century English painter John Vine commemorated it in his picture, *Sow with her Piglets*. But the paintings and photos do not convey how much preparation goes into the birth. Pigs' particularity about their environment is even more in evidence at birth time than

A sow usually gives birth to between six and fourteen piglets, although the size of litters increases with the number of pregnancies, and up to 18 newborns is not uncommon. Reports of the largest litter vary, but it seems likely to have been in the mid-30s.

Pigs lack a protein that helps other mammals keep warm, which researchers believe they lost in the past because they were living in a hot climate. To compensate, piglets shudder to keep warm.

usual. Despite the animal's typical love of society, when it comes to labor, the pig prefers solitude. The sow leaves her herd and builds a private nest both for farrowing, or birthing, her young and for protection in their early days. This is an important project for the expectant mother, and she is very precise in her specifications. Wild sows will walk up to six miles to find the right location, which must be far from other animals and well protected. Once the spot has been chosen, the nest-building itself can take as long as ten hours. When it is finished, she is ready for the rigors of labor.

Litters typically consist of six to fourteen baby piglets, but the number rises with each successive pregnancy, and it is not unusual for older sows to give birth to 18 piglets. Reports of the largest litter on record vary, but it seems likely to be somewhere in the mid-30s. An ideal number is

12, as the sow generally has 12 teats, reducing competition among her young for milk. Provided there are no complications, the delivery takes around an hour or two, with each piglet following its predecessor after a quarter or half an hour, and weighing around 6–12 ounces (170 to 340 g). Although they are born with good mobility, and can move around soon after birth, they will stick closely to their mother in the beginning. Their first priority is to feed. Survival chances are given a huge boost if the piglet has managed to nurse in its first 24 hours, as its mother's milk will be high in colostrum, which boosts the newborn's immunity. At this stage, bacteria represent a real danger for the young animals, and without their mother's protective milk they remain perilously vulnerable to infection and illness. Fortunately, in normal circumstances baby pigs soon start to feed, making their way to their mother's teats

with such determination that it usually breaks the umbilical cord. At first the piglets suckle randomly, but soon the sow institutes a more organized schedule, as she has a lot of feeding to do, with her offspring each wanting milk up to 20 times a day. Within two days, a strict nursing order will have been implemented. The sow must also take care to keep her infants warm—one reason that she spends so long perfecting her nest. For their first three days of life, baby piglets have no control over their body temperature. Pigs lack a protein that helps other mammals keep warm, which researchers believe they lost in the past because they were living in a hot climate. To compensate, baby piglets must shudder to keep warm, while in pig farming, heat lamps are used.

A sow normally produces two litters in a year. But such a high fertility rate implies a high

mortality rate—in some breeds it can reach 50 percent. Young piglets face a number of threats. In the wild, bobcats, wolves, coyotes, black bears, as well as snakes and raptors prey on baby pigs. Starvation and disease are other risks. But danger can also come from closer to home. While the sow is an attentive mother, the sheer size of her litter presents logistical problems. The task of keeping her eye on up to a dozen mobile youngsters is just not possible, and some baby pigs get squashed by their mother, who weighs over a hundred times more than they do. The size of the litter also produces competition for food. Born with eyeteeth, observers have noticed that piglets use these as weapons against their siblings when trying to secure the best teats for feeding. Faced with strong and aggressive siblings, the runt may struggle to get enough milk.

However, life with the siblings is not always brutal. Piglets spend their early days playing together amicably, although always close to their mother. For the first two weeks or so, the mother and her young will stay in the nest. Then they will make their way back to the herd for the piglets to start their education, of which play is an important element. Play-fighting, frolicking, chasing, and exploration all teach them much-needed survival skills for later in life. Cooperation and observation will also save them effort—pigs much prefer to find food by noticing that another animal in the herd has located some, rather than going to the bother of seeking it out themselves. But perhaps the

Much maligned as dirty, stupid, and greedy, even the word "pig" has come to stand as an all-purpose insult. The truth is quite different: pigs are clean and intelligent, with a diet that consists largely of water.

most important lesson is in communication. Pigs have developed a sophisticated system of conversing, which involves greetings—nose-to-nose contact and grooming—not dissimilar from our own. Sows and piglets develop unique noises to alert each other to their presence or communicate basic messages, which they can distinguish even among a cacophony of sounds from other animals. Such an advanced method of communication has been observed in no other farm or domesticated animals. Some biologists believe that the animals can recognize and recall up to 30 other pigs. Their communal spirit even has them sleeping together at night, huddled in a nest in groups of up to 15 animals. Learning this lesson of togetherness, newborn piglets become part of the herd. The males will eventually leave to set out alone, but the females may stay with the herd for life.

After around five weeks, solid food is introduced into the piglets' diet. By twelve weeks they are likely to have been weaned. Growth ends at around three and a half years, sometimes as late as five. But as both boars and gilts become fertile at around eight months, their own experience of parenthood may have started long before.

While many myths persist about pigs, their highly social nature does seem to have been met with recognition. That, coupled with the cuteness of their young, has established some piglets as well-known and much-loved characters in popular culture. One thing that all fictional piglets seem to have in common is innocence—often a dangerous innocence. Guilelessness proves fatal in *The Three Little Pigs*, an old tale that first appeared in print in the 18th century and then found even more fame in a Walt Disney cartoon in 1933. The story centers on three piglets who are sent to build a house for the family, but argue and instead decide to build three separate houses. The first two young pigs build weak houses of hay and sticks respectively, which are easily destroyed by the story's villain, the big bad wolf. The pigs' exchange with the wolf features dialog that is now embedded in Western culture:

Little pig, little pig, let me come in.
No, no, I won't let you come in, not by the hair on my chinny chin chin.
Then I'll huff and I'll puff and I'll blow your house in.

The third pig goes against type, builds a house of brick, and manages to boil the wolf in a pot. But this quick-thinking, ruthless piglet is not

typical of his kind's presentation. More often the pig is vulnerable and timid, like Piglet, a character from the British author A.A. Milne's *Winnie-the-Pooh* books. As he puts it himself, "'It is hard to be brave,' said Piglet, sniffing slightly, 'when you're only a Very Small Animal.'" But despite his apprehensive disposition, through the course of Milne's stories, Piglet manages to chase Woozles and Heffalumps, join an "exposition" to the North Pole, survive a flood, and rescue Pooh and Owl when they are trapped.

Piglet's triumph over his timorous nature to achieve great things is also evident in perhaps the most popular fictitious piglet of recent years, *Babe*, of the Oscar®-winning 1995 film of the same name. In an echo of the Ugly Duckling moral, Babe is a runt, who is won at a fair by Farmer Hoggett. It soon becomes evident that the piglet is a splendid sheep-herder, and must put his talents to use in a competition if he is to save the farm. The success of the movie inspired a sequel three years later, *Babe: Pig in the City*. The piglet's popularity in Western culture may well be summed up by Babe's tagline: "A Little Pig Goes a Long Way."

Pigs are very social animals, with a sophisticated system of communicating with and greeting each other. They even sleep huddled together, in groups of up to 15. While males will eventually leave the herd, females will stay for life.

Polar Bears

Having to survive in the harsh environment of the frozen Arctic, polar bear cubs must quickly learn from their mothers all that they will need to grow into strong adults.

As global warming becomes an increasingly urgent topic of public debate, the environmentalists have found a champion posterboy in the baby polar bear. In convincing people to cut down on their flights, give up their SUVs, and recycle, what better incentive than to save one of the most appealing creatures this planet has (so appealing that it is used to market the world's biggest brand)? The melting of the polar ice caps makes the polar bear one of the first, and most visible, victims of global warming. While it has not yet been added to the endangered species list, the future for the polar bear looks bleak if humans cannot—or will not—change their consumption of the world's resources.

Climate change is just one of the crises that polar bears must face, which, combined, give their cubs just a 30 percent chance of reaching the age of three—and falling. As humans, in our unquenchable thirst for oil, move into the Arctic, we encroach on the polar bear's habitat. Our oil spills, if oil gets on the bear's coat, prevent it from regulating its own body temperature—and this is in a place with some of the most hostile climatic conditions on the planet. And the thinning ice pack, where polar bears hunt, forces them to return to the shore long before they have mustered enough food to see them through hibernation. Pollution, poaching, and industry also contribute to the animal's plight.

The polar bear has become the poster boy for the environmentalists leading the campaign against climate change. In an increasingly hostile world, polar bear cubs now have just a 30 percent chance of reaching the age of three.

The future for the polar bear looks bleak if humans cannot—or will not—change their consumption of the world's resources.

But if any animal can rouse us to action, to prevent the damage that we're wreaking from worsening, then the polar bear is it. Take Knut. He went from being a normal cub from Berlin Zoo to an international media sensation. Born in December 2006, he was rejected by his mother. Such a fate in the wild almost inevitably spells death. But instead, zookeeper Thomas Doerflein began to bring up the abandoned bear, feeding him from a bottle. This drew criticism from animal rights activists, who said that Knut should not be hand-reared, which was akin to being brought up as a domestic pet, and should instead be killed. The public outcry at this caught the eye of the media and turned the animal into an international celebrity. Visitor numbers at the zoo were double the usual figures, and the institution's stock price reached a record level. Fans followed Knut's progress on television and over the internet. His photograph was taken by renowned American portrait photographer Annie Leibovitz, and appeared on the cover of *Vanity Fair,* in a montage with Leonardo DiCaprio. A pop song has been written about him. And in true celebrity style, Knut also received death threats—thought to be a hoax, lampooning the animal rights activists' calls for him to be killed—and subsequently got his own security detail.

But Knut was not the first incursion of polar bear cubs into the media spotlight. They were already the stars of a long-running advertising campaign for Coca-Cola. Since they first appeared in commercials for the soft drink in 1993, the bears have been one of the company's biggest commercial hits, and other companies have also adopted the image of polar bears to promote their products. While the Coke ads were strong on heartwarming sweetness, commitment to accuracy seemed less of a priority: the polar bears were depicted with penguins, when the birds are confined almost exclusively to the Southern Hemisphere and polar bears to the Northern Hemisphere.

Although the climate that bears endure is harsh, the animals are well adapted to it. At conception, the polar bear's fertilized egg is subject to delayed implantation, which ensures that, regardless of precisely when mating took place, the cub's birth is timed to give it the best odds for survival. After mating, the male departs, leaving the female to look for a maternity den, to protect her newborns from winter. Typically she will have two cubs at a time, and then not mate again for three years, or in some cases two. The

In spring, the new family emerges from its hideaway, but spends the first couple of weeks nearby, sleeping and spending a lot of time inside. This allows the cubs a gentle baptism—they can gradually get used to the cold and improve their walking skills.

low birth rate—one of the slowest reproductive rates of any mammal—is one factor behind the bear's precarious position. At birth, the cubs weigh around a pound (450 g) and are so small they can fit in their mother's paw. Born blind, deaf, and helpless, they are totally reliant on mom. It takes a day for the newborn to hear, a week for it to open its eyes, and several weeks before it can move around. In the bitter northern Arctic, heat is also vital for the newborns. The mother obliges through her fur, fat, and crevices into which her tiny cubs can press for warmth. Baby polar bears' inaugural steps are taken in the den. By the time they begin walking, their first teeth will be coming through, and the fine white hair they had at birth—giving them the appearance of being bald—will be replaced by thicker fur. In spring, the new family emerges from their hideaway, although for the next couple of weeks they will stay nearby, sleeping and spending a lot of time inside. This allows the cubs a gentle baptism—they can gradually get used to the cold and improve their walking skills. Finally, they are ready to leave the security of the den, and make their first family outing to the sea ice. It is slow going. The cubs cannot yet cover long distances without frequent rest periods and feeding breaks. At times the snow and water gets too much, and the mother will carry her young on her back.

The end of this epic journey is celebrated with the baby polar bears' introduction to solid food: their mother's first kill on the sea ice. A diet of

seal blubber and milk helps them grow rapidly. Cubs will suckle for at least a year and a half, and sometimes much longer—initially for most of the time, then up to six times a day, then less frequently. Polar bear milk is by far the highest in fat of any other bear secretion, comparable to that of other marine mammals. Even after they are weaned, the cubs remain with the female—until they are chased away by her or her mate in preparation for the conception of new siblings. As well as feeding them, she must teach them to hunt, a skill which few master until they reach the age of one. As they grow, they will spend increasing amounts of time hunting. Play is another important activity. Through play-fighting and wrestling, throwing and manipulating snow and ice, they learn the skills

they will need as hunters—and hunted. Although polar bears are at the top of the Arctic food chain, they still face danger, from their own kind. The female must keep her young safe from adult males, who have been known to cannibalize baby cubs. If her offspring are threatened, the mother will have no compunction about laying down her life for them.

Rabbits

As everyone knows, rabbits are capable of having many, many children.

If there is one baby animal in no imminent danger of extinction, it must be the rabbit. Its reproductive capacity is legendary, and gave rise to the phrase "breeding like rabbits" to convey a high sex drive and rate of fertility. Capable of producing three or four litters a year of, in some species, up to an unimaginable 16 babies at a time, able to get pregnant not just on the same day as giving birth, but even while still pregnant, being "in heat" all the time—a female rabbit, or doe, as they are known, is certainly one of the most prolific matriarchs in all the animal kingdom, each one capable of producing countless descendants. But whereas any creature that is teetering on the brink of extinction or endangerment earns human sympathy, the rabbit is so successful a species that our relationship with it is more ambivalent. It is cute, but it is not vulnerable. Why, some ask, should we worry about something that is so obviously capable of looking after itself? Perhaps this thinking explains why we relate to the rabbit in several different—and opposing— ways. It is a rare example of a creature treated as food, pet, and pest, all by the same culture.

How can the same animal be so loved by a family in a domestic setting, yet poisoned as vermin elsewhere? The answer lies in the food chain. Nature could not allow one species to become too numerous. Time and again, scientists have meddled in the food chain with unforeseen consequences—one species depriving another

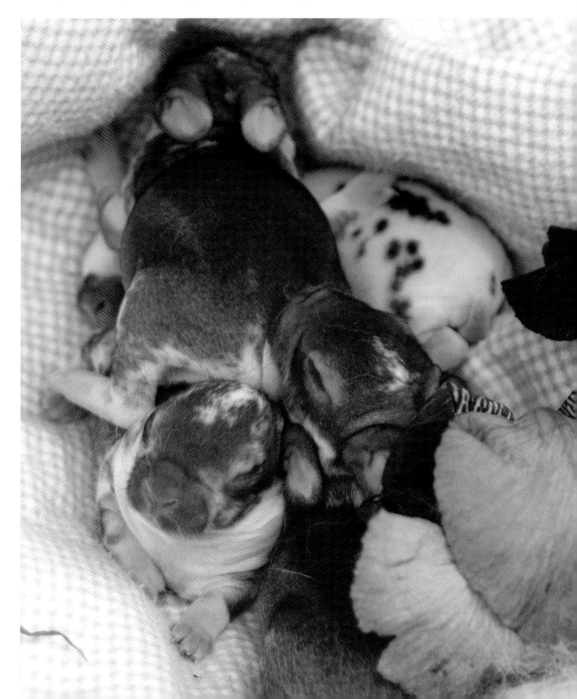

With the Australian topography offering few predators, the rabbit population exploded. There followed a rabbit rampage, with the animals stripping vast swathes of the land of vegetation.

Rabbits are well known for their reproductive capacities: capable of producing three or four litters a year of up to 16 babies at a time, able to conceive again while pregnant already, the female rabbit is one of the most prolific matriarchs in all the animal kingdom.

of its nourishment, some populations plunging, others consequently surging. And people have often had to bear the brunt to such mistakes. But humankind does not always act deliberately—negligence can be enough to upset the delicately balanced food chain and propel one species into the role of arch-villain. In Australia, when pet rabbits managed to escape the confines of their homes, disaster ensued. Elsewhere, rabbit populations are kept in check by a large number of creatures, such as foxes, badgers, and birds of prey. But with the Australian topography offering few such predators, the rabbit population exploded. There followed a rabbit rampage, with the animals stripping vast swathes of the land of vegetation. Once humans' sources of food are threatened, sympathy quickly wanes, and Australian officials took action to control the population, exterminating the creatures by poison and virus.

The high birth rate is also offset by an equivalent rabbit mortality. Although cottontails, the most widely distributed species in the United States, can live up to two years, in regions where there are plenty of predators, few get beyond their first birthday. Around 85 percent of rabbits are said to perish annually, including a third of babies. Besides predators, weather represents

Rabbits are born blind and hairless with their ears back. A week will pass before they develop a proper coat, and it can take around 10 days before their eyes open.

a danger. Severe rain can flood rabbit nests. Humans—even those with the best intentions—can also jeopardize baby rabbits' chances of survival. Happening upon a nest of bunnies waiting for their mother to return from seeking food, people often erroneously assume that the babies have been abandoned, and take it upon themselves to remove the young rabbits from the nest and hand rear them. Despite their best efforts, only one in ten of the babies is likely to make it.

The mother's absence from the nest may look like maternal neglect to human eyes, but it is in fact an essential self-defense strategy. Her presence is a sure sign to predators of vulnerable babies in the vicinity, and for that reason she will only make daily, or twice daily, nursing visits to her newborn. This vulnerability is exacerbated because rabbits are born blind and hairless with their ears back. A week will pass before they develop a proper coat, and it can take around 10 days before their eyes

open. Early days are spent in the nest, a shallow depression in the ground which the mother lines with grass and her own fur. An old woodchuck hole is ideal for the purpose; otherwise the doe has to scrape it out herself. Upon her departure, she camouflages the nest with leaves and grass, hoping to dupe both malevolent predators and benevolent humans into seeing no telltale signs of lapine life.

Gestation takes about a month. The timing of the pregnancy depends on the climate. In much of the United States, cottontails breed when the weather is fairly warm, between February and September or October. In the hotter southern states, rabbits breed all year round. Unlike many other animals, the doe does not have periods of being in heat, but can mate at any time she wishes. Ovulation is triggered by exposure to the male, or buck. After mating, he will play no further part in raising the young; indeed, he is likely to have fathered several litters by different does. Litter size depends on the species, size, and individual

The rabbit is a rare example of a creature treated as food, pet, and pest, all by the same culture. Loved as a domestic animal by some and a delicacy by others, when released into the wild the rabbit's breeding patterns can wreak havoc on the food chain.

rabbit. Small breeds, like the Netherland Dwarf, a popular pet rabbit, usually give birth to one to four babies, or kittens, as they are known, although a larger animal might mother as many as six or seven. Bigger rabbits, including the New Zealand, French Lop, Checkered, and Flemish Giants, routinely produce between an impressive 10 and 16 offspring in one pregnancy.

This amounts to a lot of feeding time. Fortunately for the doe, her babies' demands are not as great as some other mammals'. Five minutes, once a day, is usually enough to sate her newborns, thanks to the richness of her milk. But as the young grow, so do their energy needs, and when they start moving around, the mother will increase the nursing time. A doe nurses by standing over her young, while they lie on their backs. The timing of weaning is a delicate balancing of the needs of the babies and those of their mother. From four weeks of age, rabbits lose the immunity provided by the female, and ideally should continue to nurse for another two to four weeks. But it is nursing, rather than the labor or the birth itself, that takes the greatest toll on the doe, and she is happily relived of the duty. By weaning the babies one or two at a time, the doe's milk dries up slowly. At this point, the bunnies are not yet half of their full adult size.

For the does, their rest may be short-lived. Female rabbits are capable of conceiving the

same day as they give birth, and there have been cases of a mother being impregnated by a son while still nursing. Pregnancies may even overlap, with the doe conceiving a second litter while still carrying the first, in a phenomenon called "superfetation." But this kind of unadvisable

Female rabbits are capable of conceiving the same day as they give birth.

The enormous rate of reproduction of the rabbit has established it as a symbol of fertility, and the animal plays an important role in our culture and customs.

breeding can harm both mother and young. At four weeks of age, kittens are still in need of their mother's attention and milk, and the arrival of a new batch of siblings at such a crucial time of development can result in neglect. While a doe may reach sexual maturity within a few months, if she conceives too early she may be unprepared to take care of the litter, her maternal instinct not yet ready to awaken. Her pregnancy may even prove fatal. Waiting too long presents its own problems, as a doe that conceives late in life may suffer complications. Generally, in safe conditions, female rabbits have a fertility window of four years, which, given their reproductive rates, can result in a lot of babies.

But while their enormous rates of reproduction have proved troublesome for humans in some situations, they have also established the rabbit as a symbol of fertility, and the animal plays an important role in our culture and customs. Spring and Easter are synonymous with the Easter Bunny. In mythology, Eostre, the Anglo-Saxon goddess of spring from whose name the term Easter is said to have developed, saved a frozen bird by turning it into a rabbit. Because the animal used to be a bird, it could lay eggs, which is believed to have given rise to the character of the Easter Bunny, who hides eggs away for children to find in the traditional Easter egg hunt. The rabbit's common status as prey also has resonance for Easter, with its associations of innocence and sacrifice. But this victim status has also been turned on its head, with young rabbits depicted as courageous and daring, most notably in the classic 1972 novel *Watership Down*, by English novelist Richard Adams. Funny, sad, and frightening, the book became a children's classic, was translated into upwards of 20 languages and was later turned into an animated movie and TV series. Although we cast them as pets, pests and food, bunnies retain the power to inspire.

Bunnies spend much of their early life alone— not due to maternal neglect, but as an essential survival strategy: the sight of the mother alerts predators to the presence of vulnerable babies; therefore she restricts her nursing visits to once or twice daily.

Seals

These animals are clumsy on land and yet come into their own in the water, gliding through icy seas, evading predators and catching fish.

The plight of baby seals, with their beauty and vulnerability, killed for their pelts to meet demand from the fashion industry, has provided animal rights campaigners with some of their most shocking images in recent times.

Few activists illustrate the passionate dedication to their cause that some animals rights campaigners do. Risking their wellbeing and liberty, they have resorted to radical measures to get their point across. One of the milder forms of persuasion tools they have used is emotive and shocking photos of animals suffering. But in all the animal rights campaigns of recent years, few images have become as iconic as the disturbing pictures of baby seals being clubbed to death for their pelts. Photos and footage shocked readers and audiences around the world, and the backlash against the culling—and the fur trade it supplied—was powerful. But as the images were replaced in the press and faded from the public consciousness, many people assumed that the practice was now obsolete. This is far from the case. Fur's gradual return to fashion revived the demand, and baby seal hunting continues. The issue also highlights the clash of values between the modern and traditional world. Many seal hunters are native Inuit, carrying on the customs that have been handed down in their community over generations, and cultural sensitivities make many in the Western world feel uncomfortable about imposing their values on a people with such a different way of life.

On top of the hunting, the seal now faces a further threat from humankind. Global warming is devastating the mammal's natural habitat. As the ice of the polar regions melts, baby seals—who lack the swimming skills and insulation of adults—are being forced into the sea, where they drown. Freak weather conditions have left many vulnerable seal cubs at the mercy of the elements. Strong winds can prevent them from reaching their usual feeding grounds, putting them at risk of starvation. Many get into difficulties or perish in storms and tidal waves, and as the melting ice drives female seals toward increasingly unorthodox—and unsafe—breeding grounds, such catastrophes are becoming more common.

The human threat faces a mammal that must already endure life in some of earth's most hostile conditions, the Arctic and Antarctica.

The human threat faces a mammal that must already endure life in some of earth's most hostile conditions, the Arctic and Antarctica. The female seal, or cow, as she is called, takes every measure to give her offspring the best odds of endurance. One trick she uses is delayed implantation, where the embryo does not plant immediately in the uterus, but is kept in a state of dormancy. In this way, regardless of the precise moment of conception, the young will be born at a particular time, the optimum time for survival. Some animals, such as the harp seal, give birth in large groups. Seals almost always deliver one sole cub. Rearing it takes a huge amount of personal resources from the mother, and to bring up twins would be too much. Most baby seals start out life helpless. They cannot swim, they have no blubber to insulate themselves, nor are their coats waterproof. With great self-sacrifice, the mother feeds her cub, sometimes doubling or tripling its weight while she goes without. A mother fur seal does not eat for the first month of her newborn's life, by which time her ribs are clearly visible while her cub continues its growth spurt. The rich maternal milk—which contains around 60 percent fat—is vital, as fat is the only thing protecting the seal from the freezing conditions.

A cub's early days consist of little else apart from eating and sleeping. Even when mother and infant go on their first outing, they will stick close together. If the cow enters the water she will pop her head up again sporadically to check on her baby. There is nobody else to do it, as male seals, or bulls, play no part in rearing their cubs. Some baby seals cannot even count on maternal attention for too long. Just two weeks into its life, a baby harp seal is abandoned by its mother, who will abruptly stop feeding her offspring and depart Canada for Greenland, leaving her cub to make the same journey without her. Initially afraid, and crying out for their mothers, the forsaken babies congregate on the ice pack, until it starts to come apart. It is a sharp, but effective, introduction to adulthood. Soon the young seals are feeding and swimming independently—and very proficiently, reaching speeds of 16 feet (5 m) a second.

Other cubs enjoy a much longer infancy. For the first six weeks of their lives, cape fur seals can neither swim nor find their way home, and their coats have yet to become waterproof. Their exclusive food source for six months is their mothers' milk, which they will continue to feed on for another four to nine months. A precious resource, the cow does not want to waste her milk on the wrong infant. Early bonding allows the mother to learn her own cub's smell and sound. If the two are prematurely separated, before she has had time to commit her baby's identifying characteristics to memory, she may refuse to feed the young seal. Meanwhile, some pups exploit the system, suckling not only from their own mother but also from other lactating females in the area. There is significant difference within species for early skill mastery. Like elephant and cape fur seals, harp seal pups take time to learn to swim. Baby harp seals are referred to as "beaters," owing to how their flippers flail in the water during their early attempts to paddle and stay afloat. Harbor seals, by contrast, can both swim and dive from the outset.

But even the most hardy, capable seal cubs face a daunting struggle for survival. Orphaning, separation from, or a failure of recognition by the mother and trampling by careless bulls combine to determine a mortality rate of around 15 percent at a teeming breeding ground. This is before humankind plays its lethal part. As fur gradually loses its social taboo, seal hunting looks likely to continue, despite the voices of a plethora of scientists, activists, and celebrities arguing for the protection of baby seals, some of whom are just weeks old when they face a brutal death at the hands of hunters. Whether their fate comes in the form of a club, or the more indirect destruction of their habitat, the future looks like a cold place for baby seals.

Most baby seals start out life helpless. They cannot swim, they have no blubber to insulate themselves, nor are their coats waterproof.

Sheep

The common sheep, and its young lambs are a common site in farming communities around the world. The bleating of lambs is one of the most distinctive sounds of spring and signals the beginning of the season of renewal.

Picture a lamb, and you mostly likely call to mind a carefree creature, frolicking in a green meadow. It is an image infused with innocent delight. If there is anything to fear, any impending doom, the lamb is unaware of it. This innocence has been associated with lambs for centuries, and they have a potent religious symbol not just in Christianity, but also in even older faiths, encapsulating the spirit of spring and sacrifice.

The linking of lambs and spring has an obvious basis, as the animals come into the world at exactly the same time when new plants and grasses are emerging, in the Northern hemisphere between March and June, depending on the species and climate. The typical gestation period for a sheep is five or six months, although some variation is

A lamb's early days are its more precarious, with over four fifths of lamb deaths taking place in the first two or three days of life, due to starvation, hypothermia, and scours. Nursing in the first eight hours give a newborn a huge health boost.

not uncommon. Although the animals are well-known for their tendency to flock together, they show no such inclination when it comes to labor: ewes seek solitude for the process of giving birth. This holds for both the wild and domesticated versions. Wild mountain sheep will leave their small groups, or bands, which consist of ewes and their young, to find a private spot for delivery. Isolation and protection are at a premium, and the ewe often seeks out a high, rocky ledge or a cave. While a domestic sheep does not have the luxury of choosing precisely where she will go into labor, she usually manages to secure herself a degree of privacy through the timing of the birth—many lambs are born around 3 or 4 o'clock in the morning, when there is the least chance of any unwelcome intrusion. From beginning to end, labor lasts about three hours. Multiple births, of up to three lambs, are frequent. However, more lambs also come with a chance of more complications. Twins and triplets are at risk of getting tangled, or attempting to be born simultaneously. Even a lone lamb, if it is too big for its mother's pelvic area, can cause problems, and sometimes has to be sacrificed for the sake of its mother.

Shortly after birth, the mother expels the placenta, some of which she may nibble on, as it is high in nutrition. The first hours are crucial for the establishment of a strong emotional attachment between the female sheep and her young. When the baby emerges from the amniotic sac, the ewe will set about licking her newborn clean. Not only does this have a practical purpose, cleaning and drying the lamb, and therefore keeping it warm, the procedure is also a bonding ritual. Should there be more

Immediately following birth, the newborn is helpless, although it usually manages to get shakily to its feet within half an hour.

The lamb has long been a symbol of springtime and innocence, with religious and spiritual associations that pre-date Christianity. The creature was also used as a sacrifice in Biblical times, giving rise to the expression "the sacrificial lamb."

than one newborn, they will likely be cleaned in the order in which they emerged. Immediately following birth, the newborn is helpless, although it usually manages to get shakily to its feet within half an hour. In the domestic setting, breeders are advised to avoid separating the female and young if at all possible. If the lamb has to be removed from its mother, the ewe may get confused about the number of babies she produced. Left together, the ewe will form a powerful connection with her young, and each learns to recognize the other by smell and sound. This time is equally important for the lamb's health. Over four fifths of lamb deaths take place in the first two or three days of life, with starvation, hypothermia, and scours, a type of diarrhea, the main dangers. The lamb's first eight hours of life are a vital window to safeguard its future health. In that time its body is highly receptive to the antibodies present in its mother's colostrum. From eight hours onwards,

its capacity to absorb antibodies efficiently slumps. Without these antibodies, its defense against infant diseases is considerably depleted. Fortunately, the lamb has an instinctive urge to seek milk, and the female will help her uncertain newborn along. Any hesitation, and the ewe will prompt it with a gentle nudge or prod, and guide it towards her udder. By the time an hour has passed, the newborn is usually happily feeding. For a few weeks, the baby lamb will nurse once or twice an hour, for up to three minutes at a time. After a month, the frequency of feeding falls to once every couple of hours.

By this time, the new family is back with the band. They will have spent only the first few days alone, before returning to the security of group living, and all the protection that it affords. With few natural gifts to defend themselves, sheep rely on the principle of safety in numbers. Humans are not the only species

Like many babies, lambs enjoy their sleep, indulging in shuteye for up to 12 hours a day, always close to their mother.

who enjoy lamb meat. In the wild, sheep have to protect their young from the attentions of bears, wolves, and birds of prey such as golden eagles. Faced with such foes as well as the ever present threat of disease, many lambs will not survive their first year.

But despite the hazards, infancy for lambs can often be as gay and carefree as our popular images of them suggest. Like many babies, they enjoy their sleep, indulging in shuteye for up to 12 hours a day, always close to their mother. When awake, they are sociable and curious, gamboling with their fellow lambs and exploring their new habitat. They run, prance, and play piggyback with mom. Along with play comes education. The ewes in the group must ensure that their charges develop the appropriate feeding behavior, and know well how to avoid danger. Lambs are blessed with neither great speed nor strength, and are unlikely to emerge victorious from a tussle with a wolf, bear, or eagle. Summer, then, is the learning season for lambs,

Ewes form a powerful bond with their young in the time immediately following the birth, and the two learn to recognize each other by smell and sound; for this reason separating them too soon can have damaging consequences.

who study in the safety of the group. When fall comes, it brings greater independence, as the lambs will be weaned. At this stage, they weigh ten times as much as when they were newborns. Winter provides another test, not only for the young lambs but also for the next, as yet unborn, generation. Some animals may not have grown sufficiently to survive the hostile winter climate. Meanwhile, embryonic lambs are also being shaped by the outside climate. If the food supply is affected, or if the conditions produce inclement spring weather, the pregnancy suffers. With the arrival of spring, the lambs look forward to their first birthday—an important milestone on the road to survival and adult life. Even so, they are not yet ready to go it alone. Females in the wild will never leave their group, which interacts with males only for breeding. But the males will eventually go their own way, usually between the ages of two and four. They will form their own bands with other young rams, pursue ewes, and the circle of life will begin again.

Life and death—both are vital elements of our associations with the lamb. Much of the animal's symbolism in our culture today derives from a faith basis. The Ancient Egyptians are thought to have been the first to have adopted the lamb into their religious iconography. It is also a common reference in Judaism and Christianity, where it is frequently representative of innocence and sacrifice. The Roman catacombs include many frescoes on the theme. The Passover lamb was the innocent animal whose blood was spilled and daubed above the front doors of the houses of Israel. Once done, the Angel of Death would pass over the house, rather than coming to claim the firstborn. Today, Jews commemorate the event with the ritual feast of Passover Seder, although the practice was not confirmed to this one event and was a standard custom in Biblical times. A lamb is also present in the Nativity, its own innocence reflecting that of the newborn baby. The sacrificial lamb is a popular motif throughout the Bible. Like the Passover lamb, it suffered for the sake of others. Jesus is frequently compared with a sacrificial lamb, as in the Biblical verse: "Behold the Lamb

of God, which taketh away the sin of the world!" (John 1:29), and pictures of the lamb, symbolizing Christ, are on display in many homes throughout Central and Eastern Europe. Much of this centers on Easter customs. In previous centuries, it was considered lucky to meet a lamb, particularly at Easter, as it was thought that although the devil could take many forms, he could not appear as a lamb due to its religious significance. These associations made lamb meat a popular choice for Easter celebrations. In today's phraseology, a "sacrificial lamb" is typically a person whose own fate, career, or reputation is forfeited for the

good of an organization or higher-ups. Meekness is another quality encapsulated by the young animal. The lion lying down with the lamb is a potent religious vision, a symbol of the whole of creation living in peace, strong and weak, without fear or aggression. But this use of the animal in religious imagery is unusual—typically the lamb faces, sometimes unwittingly, an early death. This association is summed up in the simile "like a lamb to the slaughter," to describe someone who is blithely unconcerned, unaware of the impending catastrophe. Again, the origins are Biblical. Jeremiah 11:19 reads: "But I was like

a gentle lamb led to the slaughter; And I did not know that they had devised plots against me, [saying,] 'Let us destroy the tree with its fruit, And let us cut him off from the land of the living, That his name be remembered no more.'" The comparison occurs again in Isaiah 57:3, which reflects the lamb's inability to escape its fate: "He was oppressed, and he was afflicted, yet he opened not his mouth: he is brought as a lamb to the slaughter, and as a sheep before her shearers is dumb, so he openeth not his mouth." The lamb as a symbol of the death of a young or innocent being was embraced by the Victorians in England, who used it as the most common symbol to mark a child's grave. The many cultural, symbolic, and religious associations of the lamb with death and suffering cast a sad specter over our happy image of a young animal, gaily exploring the flourishing world.

Tigers

The jungles of India are home to one of the most beautiful creatures on earth. The tiger has a distinctive camouflage allowing it to stalk its prey; a unique attribute passed down from generation to generation.

A pregnant tigress cuts a lonely and vulnerable figure. Unlike the lioness, she has no one to help feed her in the latter stages of pregnancy, when attack and starvation become real threats. Evolution has responded to her plight by giving her a relatively short gestation period of around 100 days. In the lead-up to labor, she will seek a well-protected, safe, and hidden area, such as a cave, ledge, or among dense vegetation. An extra measure of privacy comes from the timing, with most tiger births taking place at night. She delivers her litter with a minimum of fuss, with ten or twenty minutes between each cub, and the whole thing is normally over in an hour (although in captivity it can take much longer, with an 18-hour birth having been observed). Thereupon her solitude is shattered by a litter of between one and seven cubs, the average being two to four, all of them blind. The mother's first task is to break the umbilical cord and lick each baby clean. In the wild, food resources are too precious to waste, and she will feed on the cord, embryonic sac, and placenta. The blind newborns must then use their mother's body heat to find a teat and begin nursing, a challenge which typically takes between one and four hours. And here is their first lesson in life's Darwinian harshness: The mother will do nothing to help them. In the precarious existence of the tiger, a poorly adapted cub is too much of a burden, and the tigress cannot be soft-hearted. If the cub finds the teat, it will pound it to stimulate milk production. If it fails to do so—it dies. Infant

Unlike lions, tiger cubs do not enjoy the protection of an extended group; the father plays no part in protecting his mate or offspring, leaving the pregnant or new mother tigress isolated and vulnerable to attack and starvation.

> *One good safety mechanism for cubs is to be female. The males, bigger and bolder, start to venture off alone from about a year old. Not all return. For cubs, fortune seldom favors the brave.*

mortality is not shocking in the tiger kingdom. The runt, or weakest sibling, even if it avoids starvation and crushing, will be a beacon for predators once out in the open.

At 18 inches (45 cm) in length and weighing two or three pounds (1–1.3 kg), the cubs are less than two percent of their eventual weight. Though it might seem a disadvantage, their early blindness is in fact useful, preventing them from moving around too much and attracting the attentions of predators while the mother is off hunting and the young are vulnerable. While their eyes open in three to five days, they see poorly for the first couple of months, and so stay around the den. As the bewildered cubs take in their new environment, so too is their mother adapting to her new situation. Tigresses are not natural first-time mothers, and it may take them a litter or two to get over their initial awkwardness. When they do, they will be fearsomely protective matriarchs. But even so, mortality rates among cubs in the wild are high. At least half will not live to see their second birthday, and some researchers believe that on average just one cub per litter reaches adulthood. This is partly due to the pressures of single parenthood. Fathers play no role in raising their young, and other adult males may even kill young cubs, to make the mother receptive to mating. The animal's solitary nature—aside from young families, all tigers live alone—deprives her young of the network of support an orphaned lion cub would enjoy in the event of the mother's death. Lone cubs are a tempting meal for wild dogs, hyenas, jackals, and snakes such as the python. Humankind, too, contributes to the high cub mortality rate, both directly, through poaching, and indirectly, when the fires started by farmers to ready land for grazing rage out of control, devastating the tiger's habitat. One good safety mechanism for cubs is to be female. The males, bigger and bolder, start to venture off alone from about a year old. Not all return. For cubs, fortune seldom favors the brave.

In her ceaseless battle to keep her young safe, the tigress will frequently move dens, transporting her helpless young by gripping their loose neck skin between her teeth. Their silence is imperative on this risky venture. The slightest cry could attract the attentions of a predator—including their own father. The mother is alert and primed throughout this journey, and it would be a hapless and most unfortunate creature that got in her way at this time. In this period of their life, cubs are guarded continuously—with the exception of during their mother's hunting forays. They will enjoy their first taste of the meat she snares at around two months old,

although they will continue to nurse for another four months, with weaning happening slowly. Meanwhile, cubs are also learning the skills by which they will eventually provide their own meat. Initially, this happens through play-fighting among themselves, stalking their mother's tail, and hunting small prey. Afterwards comes hunting school, headed by their mother. From observation only, the next stage will see the female injure her prey and deliver it to the young to finish off. They do not immediately take to the task. Cubs lack the lethal final blow of adults, and either start feeding on the hapless victim before

it has been killed or sometimes dither, allowing the injured animal to snatch freedom from the jaws of death and bolt. The final stage sees cubs hunt alone, graduating from birds, rodents, and fawns to larger prey. But their instincts and skills are still limited, and many meet their deaths in unwise confrontations with bigger animals. While tigers lack the solidarity of lions in many respects, in one they are more altruistic mothers, letting their young feed before they do, as opposed to the lion order of adults first, which sometimes results in lion cubs starving. Even when ravenous, the tigress prioritizes her babies' stomachs.

Increasingly competent hunters, at one and a half or two, the young are finally ready for independent life. Her next litter will once again require solitude, safety, and plentiful sources of food, so the tigress must put some distance between the siblings. She owes her newborns that if they are to have a shot—and it is a long shot—of reaching adulthood and then parenthood themselves.

Although cubs learn their rudimentary hunting and self-defense skills through play fighting, it takes a while before they attain the ruthless streak of adult tigers. Many a hopeless prey is gifted a last gasp chance of survival by an inept cub hunter.

Whales

The largest animal on earth gives birth to live young, and so must quickly teach its calf to survive in the oceans. Mother and child share a unique bond which ensures the best chance of survival.

Across most species, babies are endearing mainly because of their size. Small features connote vulnerability, which arouses our instinctive feelings of protectiveness. So it is hard for us to conceive of a newborn baby being as long as four adult humans, standing one on top of the other, and weighing as much as a tank. But such is the case for the baby blue whale, making it the largest newborn in the world.

Dimensions aside, whale breeding does not differ markedly from that of many other mammals. Polygamous creatures, whales do not have exclusive partnerships and the female, known as a cow, will take a number of different mates in order to optimize her conception chances. Mating and birthing times vary depending on the species, region, and weather, although among some creatures spring is the favored season for mating. Gestation lasts anywhere between

A calf usually starts to swim immediately—being born a mammal in the ocean it has little choice—but if it hesitates its mother will nudge it gently upwards to the surface.

10 months for the minke whale (a small member of the baleen group, which do not have teeth) up to 17 months for the killer whale, or orca, one of the longest pregnancy durations in the whole animal kingdom. Rearing young is time-consuming for whales. While some may reproduce again as early as a year later, this is rare, and others can wait up to a decade before a sibling is conceived. The scarcity of babies results in a strong maternal bond between cow and calf.

Births are usually tail-first, to minimize the chances of the newborn calf drowning. It must hold its breath during the delivery, and no sooner than it emerges, find its way to the top of the ocean and gasp for air. A calf usually starts to swim immediately—being born a mammal in the ocean it has little choice—but if it hesitates its mother will nudge it gently upwards to the surface. Throughout labor and afterwards, the mother may be assisted by an "aunt," another female whale who holds the mother above the water or helps the newborn to the surface. Such help is welcomed, as birthing is a dangerous time. Blood released into the sea can alert predators to the presence of a vulnerable new baby, on top of which the sea can be rough. Many gray whales prefer the calmness of the Pacific coast lagoons of Baja California, the Mexican peninsula, where the shallow, warm, predator-free, and buoyant water eases some of the concerns attendant to

The beluga, pictured on the opposite page and above, is one of the smallest newborns of the whale kingdom, about four to five feet (1.3–1.5 m) long and weighing just 100 pounds (45 kg); at the other end of the scale is the blue whale calf, as long as four people and as heavy as a tank.

the delivery. Twins are rare—slightly above or below one percent of births, depending on the species.

While the blue whale calf's size at birth is exceptionally large, other baby newborns also boast impressive dimensions. Of the baleen suborder, the smallest is the minke, who still emerges on average a foot longer than the world's tallest man, at nine feet (2.7 m). Right whales, humpbacks, bowheads, and gray whales all measure between 14 and 17 feet (4.2–5.1 m), still some way off the blue whale's immense proportions. The species' smaller babies are to be found among the toothed suborder: the beluga whale comes out at a relatively tiny four to five feet (1.3–1.5 m) and its cousin, the narwhal, is a similar size. The orca, or killer whale, is slightly larger at between 6.5 and 8 feet (2–2.6 m), with the sperm whale the largest of the group at some 13 feet (4 m). Typical birth weights range from 100 pounds (45 kg) for the beluga up to the blue whale's eight tons (7,250 kg).

Presented with her newborn, the cow's maternal instincts kick in, although first-time mothers may initially experience some reservations and uncertainty. Again, the social nature of the whale helps out: the mother will learn by observing the other females in her pod, the social unit in which whales live. While the calf can swim on its own within a few days, the cow pays close attention, never letting it stray too far. Sometimes, particularly when it feels threatened,

the calf will ride along on its mother's back. Other times, she keeps her baby close with the help of the slipstream, the reduced pressure that carries the baby along in the wake of its swimming mother. In this way the calf can keep up with the pod without its energy resources becoming too depleted. At this age, energy comes exclusively from the mother. Some babies first feed as soon as their third hour. Nursing usually takes place close to the surface of the water. The calf signals its hunger by bumping its mother, who squirts her milk into the calf's mouth. Feeding lasts for just five to ten seconds, and is repeated several times an hour throughout day and night. After peaking in the first couple of days, it reduces from a total of 90 minutes per day to about 10, along with the calf's increasing efficient consumption. Whale milk contains over 50 percent fat, and in consistency is more akin to cottage cheese than cow or human milk. It needs to be—not only would a thinner

Blue whales produce up to 160 gallons (600 liters) daily, helping their babies put on an impressive eight to ten pounds an hour, doubling their initial weight in as little as one week.

Baby whales enjoy social support outside their immediate family: births are assisted by an "aunt," another female who helps the newborn to the surface and keeps an eye out for predators who may be attracted by the blood from the delivery.

substance dissolve in the sea water, but a calf's energy needs are huge. Blue whales produce up to 160 gallons (600 liters) daily, helping their babies put on an impressive eight to ten pounds (3.6–4.5 kg)an hour, doubling their initial weight in as little as one week. Such high amounts are not limited to the largest mammal: humpback calves also put away 100 pounds (45 kg) of milk every day. Such high consumption is necessary to provide the animals' layer of blubber, a vital insulation method and energy reserve. Weaning usually happens at the end of a year, by which time the fat content of the milk will have dropped by almost half. Once a calf is weaned, and can find its own food, it is ready for independent life, although some may stay with their mothers for slightly longer.

It is hard to imagine the world's largest species of mammal having predators, but in fact baby whales face a number of dangers—some from within the whale kingdom. On their northward migration, gray whales—no more than a few weeks old—must elude the attention of orcas, who line their 5,000-mile (8,000 km) route in wait. Humans have also had a hand in their plight. Whaling, part of our culture since 6000 BC, has dramatically reduced whale populations, and put some species on the endangered list. Despite an international moratorium, exemptions and caveats allow some nations to continue the practice. But whaling is not the only industry to threaten the creatures. The intensity and speed of shipping in some areas kills or critically injures many whales. Some researchers estimate that up to half of North Atlantic right whale deaths, the most endangered whale off the United States Atlantic coast, are due to the animals being struck by fast-moving ships. The creature numbers are now in the low hundreds.

Zebras

This unique animal is a fascinating feature of the African savannah. The distinctive camouflage of the Zebra has ensured its survival in one of the world's harshest terrains.

There is little to romanticize in zebra reproduction. Instead of devoted couples, the common zebra forms harems. Instead of choosing her mate, the female is kidnapped, dragged reluctantly into membership of a new herd. But despite this unpromising start to her life as a mate and mother, the mare will inculcate a strong bond between herself and her infant, a bond that she will protect against even the lead stallion.

She certainly has a long time to get used to the idea of impending motherhood. Pregnancy in the zebra lasts around a year, sometimes longer, with no particular breeding season. After such a long gestation period, the foal emerges in a well-developed state, weighing in the region of 50 to 120 pounds (23–55 kg), depending on the species. It already has the long legs on which its later survival will depend, and its mobility develops rapidly. Within as little as 15 minutes,

The first couple of days are crucial for the newborn to learn the mare's stripes, sound, and smell. Without this crucial imprinting, the foal will follow any moving object.

the newborn will get shakily to its feet, and early attempts to run come after around an hour. In a few more hours, its long legs and increasing confidence allow it to keep up with the herd— an essential development, as without it, the foal would be perilously vulnerable. Although its safety depends to a great extent on group living and cooperation, initially the new mother will shun the attentions of the herd, keeping the other animals—including the father—away from her offspring. This is not because they pose a threat. Indeed, some species of zebra raise their young in a collaborative spirit, looking out for all the herd's young in times of strife. But the first couple of days are crucial for the newborn to learn the mare's stripes, sound, and smell. Without this crucial imprinting, the foal will follow any moving object. Nursing also starts early, often within the first hour. Although the foal's diet will expand to include grasses from a week or two old, it will continue to suckle from its mother for a year. On this nourishing milk it is just a few weeks until the baby doubles its weight.

Back among the herd, the young zebra starts to learn survival skills from its fellow animals. The foals engage in play-fighting, racing, chasing, pushing, and shoving each other—having fun but, crucially, building up their speed and strength. Despite their increasing curiosity and adventurousness, foals rarely venture too far from their mothers. Although other herdmates will look out for a foal in trouble—the lead stallion even going so far as to follow it and shepherd it back to the group if it wanders off—only the mother is fully dedicated to caring for her own young. Within one species of zebra, this relationship is even more exclusive. Unlike plains (or common) and mountain zebras, the dispersal of resources in their habitat prevents Grevy's zebras from forming small groups led by a stallion. Grevy's adults do not develop the connections with each other that keep the groups in the other two species so tightly knit, and here the only lasting bond is between mother and infant. Zebras enjoy physical contact with each other, and a mother and foal are frequently spotted grooming each other. They stand side by side—always facing in opposite directions so they have a 360-degree panoramic view of their surroundings and any potential threat—and nibble gently at each other's fur.

But young zebras must also learn another, more unusual kind of cooperation: cross-species. To bolster their defenses against the many predators who share their habitat, the animals form mixed herds with antelope and other herbivores. Speed forms the nub of a zebra's danger avoidance strategy, along with keen senses that remain alert to the slightest danger. If there is no chance of outrunning the hunter, the animals will fall back on their solidarity, circling a vulnerable foal to prevent the assailant from reaching it. They then continue to move, closely huddled together, with the stallion at the back of the group, attacking the predators and effecting the herd's escape. Lions and hyenas are the animal's main enemies, and to a lesser extent hunting dogs, leopards, and cheetahs. The cub's first year is its most dangerous. Despite its long legs, a young foal has yet to develop the speed and endurance that give it a chance of eluding the lion. Further threat comes from within— disruption in the foal's own herd. Despite the generally stable nature of the group, at some point the stallion will die or be challenged for his position by a younger, stronger animal. The new leader will suffer no competition,

Guineans once interpreted the zebra's stark black and white stripes as a symbol of the unpredictability of life.

and shows little mercy for the existing babies. In such a dire predicament, the foals cannot rely on any help from their mother, who will do nothing to prevent the infanticide, as she stands to gain the protection of the new leader and potentially better genes for her next offspring. Fortunately, lead stallions remain in place for long tenures, so such situations are rare. However, the foals must soon go their own way. Young males leave of their own accord, honing their skills in bachelor herds as a precursor to making their own attempts to take over a harem. Females are either driven out when they reach sexual maturity to prevent in-breeding, or kidnapped by other males. From parental protection to outcast or abductee—the young zebra soon learns the lessons of life's capriciousness. Aptly, Guineans once interpreted the zebra's stark black and white stripes as a symbol of this very unpredictability.

Mutual grooming, right, not only builds herd and parent-child bonds, but zebras' habit of facing in opposite directions while doing so provides them with a 360-degree panoramic view and the best chance of spotting any approaching predators.

Index